DRAMATIS PERSONAE

This is not an exhaustive list of all those involved with the project but refers mainly to those characters that feature in the book.

Competition Assessors
Sir Leslie Martin – Professor of Architecture, Cambridge University
Eero Saarinen – American architect
(with Cobden Parks and Professor Ashworth – *see below*)

Utzon's Office
Jørn Utzon
Jacob Kielland-Brandt
Helge Hjertholm
Knud Lautrup-Larsen
Jon Lundberg
Bob Maclurcan
Yuzo Mikami (1958-1961)
Rafael Moneo
Oktai Nayman
Olaf Skipper-Nielsen
Mogens Prip-Buus
James Thomas
Bill Wheatland

Hall Todd & Littlemore
(architectural consortium that replaced Utzon in 1966)
Peter Hall – Design Architect
David Littlemore
Lionel Todd

Ove Arup and Partners
Ove Arup
Povl Ahm
John Blanchard
David Croft
David Dowrick
Joe Huang
Ronald Jenkins
Bob Kelman
John Lethbridge
Michael Lewis
Ian McKenzie
David Melling
Duncan Michael
Yuzo Mikami (1961-1967)
Hugo Mollman
John Nutt
Peter Rice
Jack Zunz

Sydney Opera House Executive Committee (SOHEC)

'Silent' Stan Haviland – Chairman

Henry Ingham Ashworth – Professor of Architecture, University of Sydney

Sir Charles Moses – General Manager, Australian Broadcasting Commission (ABC)

Sir Bernard Heinze – Conductor, Sydney Symphony Orchestra (SSO)

The Contractor

Dundas Corbet Gore – Director of Construction, Hornibrook Limited

The Politicians

John 'Joe' Cahill – NSW (New South Wales) Labor Premier 1952-1959

Robert J Heffron – NSW Labor Premier 1959-1964

John B Renshaw – NSW Labor Premier 1964-1965

Norman Ryan – Labor Minister for Public Works 1959-1965

Robert J Askin – NSW Liberal Premier 1965-1975

Davis Hughes – Liberal/Country Party Coalition Minister for Public Works 1965-1973

Robert Carr – Labor Premier, 1995–

The Consultants

Rider Hunt and Partners – Quantity Surveyors

Vilhelm Lassen Jordan – Acoustics Consultant (Denmark)

Lothar Cremer – Acoustics Consultant (Berlin)

Werner Gabler – Acoustics Consultant (Berlin)

Joachim Nutsch – Acoustics Engineer (working for Cremer)

Balslev and Partners – Electrical Engineering Services

Steensen & Varming – Mechanical Services

S Malmquist – Theatre Techniques

Julius Poole & Gibson – Electrical Engineering services

The Public Works Department (PWD)

Cobden Parkes – Government Architect (1935-1958) at the time of the competition

Ted Farmer – Government Architect (1958-1973), successor to Parkes

Bill Wood – Liaison Architect

The saga of
SYDNEY OPERA HOUSE

aren't YOU proud of me...? I'm Mr. DAVIS-HUGHES, your future MINISTER FOR CULTURE... I've just achieved the greatest personal SUCCESS of my political career... in MY eyes, and I'm SURE yours... I AM a GREAT MAN...a sort of ANTIPODEAN ANDRE MALRAUX.... What a BRILLIANT move forcing that DANISH PRIMA-DONNA to resign, he'd want to sing his own BLOODY operas if we'd let him stay. We can finish that Bloody monstrosity own our own—THANK YOU! We have some of the WORLD'S GREATEST architects RIGHT HERE in Australia, WALTER BUNNING for example.... Just look at the wonderful buildings he's done... I've even drawn up a few plans meself..... BLOODY GOOD TOO...Heaven FORBID I'm no Architect.... I'm not even a Bachelor of SCIENCE.... NOW DON'T get me WRONG... I ADMIRE UTZON... GOD KNOWS I've supported the OPERA HOUSE for years now... ...buying Lottery tickets... NEVER WINNING... money out of me own pocket.... I BET those piddling ARTY Architects never bought any.... FANCY them trying to pull the merino over my pale blue deep-set, far-seeing eyes- carrying on pretending arch- -itecture is ART.... JUST WHO ARE THEY TRYING TO FOOL! —I KNOW BETTER-it's just FANCY BUILDING... MR. FARMER WILL DO A WONDERFUL JOB, JUST YOU WAIT and SEE! ...FARMER... I like that name it reminds me of the BUSH... WHERE I BELONG...

BACHELOR of SCIENCE Mr DAVIS-HUGHES HA HA.

SHARP

Cartoon by Martin Sharp for Oz magazine caricaturing Davis Hughes, NSW Minister for Public Works. 1966.

The saga of
SYDNEY OPERA HOUSE

The dramatic story of the design
and construction of the icon
of modern Australia

by Peter Murray

 Spon Press
Taylor & Francis Group

LONDON AND NEW YORK

First published 2004 by Spon Press
11 New Fetter Lane, London EC4P 4EE
Simultaneously published in the USA and Canada
by Spon Press
29 West 35th Street, New York, NY 10001

Spon Press is an imprint of the Taylor & Francis Group

Typeset in Book Antiqua by Wordsearch
Printed and bound in Great Britain by TJ International Ltd, Padstow, Cornwall

Murray, Peter, 1920-
The saga of Sydney Opera House: the dramatic story of the design and construction of the
icon of modern Australia/by Peter Murray.
164pp. 16x22 cm.
Included bibliographical references and index.
ISBN 0-415-32521-8 (hb.:alk paper)
ISBN 0-203-35816-3 (ebook)
ISBN 0-415-32522-6 (pb.: alk paper)
1. Sydney Opera House. 2. Utzon, Jørn, 1918-. 3. Sydney (N.S.W.) – Buildings, structures,
etc. I. Title.

NA6840.A79S96 2003
725'.822'099441–DC22

CONTENTS

saga /ˈsaːga/ *n.* long story of heroic achievement, esp. medieval tale
of Scandinavian heroes.

Between earth and sky
It's here you live and here you die
And the spirit of man
Is torn between
The earth he knows
And the sky he's seen

The Eighth Wonder, an opera by Alan John and Dennis Watkins
about the construction of the Opera House.

PREFACE

In 1966, as Editor of the student section of *The Architect's Journal*, I commissioned a drawing by Martin Sharp of Oz magazine which caricatured a grotesque Australian politician boasting of having forced the Danish architect Jørn Utzon to resign from the Sydney Opera House (page ii). Sharp's critical and incisive view of the Opera House affair, describing the philistine destruction of genius, was to stay with me for the next 35 years.

However, as I researched the design and construction of the Opera House an altogether more complex and difficult story than the one encapsulated in Sharp's cartoon began to emerge.

I have dug through archival papers that have not been read for 35 years, read oral histories that have only become accessible after the author's death and had access to unpublished personal accounts written by some of the leading protagonists. I have studied the mass of information and drawings that are available in archives in Sydney and in the UK. Such a complex story, made up of a series of intertwining tales, is hard to tell in chronological order. However I have attempted to do so in order to give as close a reflection as possible of the actual events.

I have spoken to many people about the project who have been very helpful in the preparation of the text. My thanks are particularly due to Jack Zunz, David Messent, Bill Wheatland, Marit Tronslin, Ian Patrick, Harry and Penelope Seidler, James France, Martin Sharp, Derek Sugden, Bob Essling, Anne Minors, Hannah Weir, Sutherland Lyall, Warwick Mehaffey, Minty Smyth, Rob Dusting, Brian Perry, Trevor Dannatt, Andy Dunican, James Thomas, Professor Bjorn Peterssen, Anthony Blee, Anne Kriken, John Rourke, Michael Taylor, Martin the driver for West Bus in Penrith, the staff at the Mitchell Library and, of course, my long-suffering family.

In any story such as this, the tale can be told from a variety of angles. Each version may be true, but it will be different in tone and in its views of the outcome. I have set out the facts from contemporary papers and accounts as I found them. The reader can, with the benefit of hindsight, imagine how they might have acted in similar circumstances.

Peter Murray
Bedford Park
May 2003

Supporting Cast

Eugene Goossens – Conductor, Sydney Symphony Orchestra 1947-1957

Walter Bunning – Australian Architect

Harry Seidler – Viennese-born Australian Architect

Elias Duek-Cohen – Architect, Lecturer and Associate Professor, University of New South Wales

Ralph Symonds – Ralph Symonds Limited, Plywood Manufacturer

Steen Eiler Rasmussen – Danish Architectural Writer and Teacher

Os Jarvis – Australian Architect

Talbot Duckmanton – General Manager, ABC, in succession to Moses

Warwick Mehaffey – Acoustics Engineer, ABC

Peter Miller – Engineer, Miller Milston and Ferris

Ron Gilling – President, New South Wales Chapter of the Royal Australian Institute of Architects (RAIA)

Philip Nobis – Australian Architect

Richard Johnson – appointed 1998 as Architect for the 25-year SOH masterplan

IMPORTANT DATES

1957

Jan 29   Competition result announced.
          Cost estimate A£3.5million (A$7million).
Mar 21   Utzon agrees to work with Ove Arup.
July 29   Utzon in Sydney for the first time.

1958

Mar 26   Utzon in Sydney with the Red Book.
          Cost estimate A£4,812,000 (A$9,624,000).
Mar 31   Premier Cahill insists work is started in February 1959.
          Project divided into three phases: Stage 1 – platform,
          Stage 2 – roof shells, tiling, Stage 3 – walls and interiors.

1961

Sept 20   Estimate: A£9,300,000 (A$18,600,000).
Oct   Utzon decides to base the geometry of the shells on that
          of a sphere.

1962

Jan   Yellow Book submitted.
Apr   Estimated cost: A£13,750,000 (A$27,500,000).
Dec 26   Boxing Day meeting with Arups at Heathrow, before Utzon
          and family leave on journey to Australia.

1963

Mar 4   Monday: Utzon flies in to Sydney.
Mar 25   Hornibrook commence work on Stage 2.
Apr 5   Arup Engineer Michael Lewis arrives in Sydney on crutches
          after a bus accident at Tel Aviv.
Sept   Estimated cost A£14,799,529 (A$29,599,058).

1964

Feb 26   Receivers appointed to Ralph Symonds Ltd.

Apr 1   Estimated cost: A£17,200,000 (A$34,400,000).

1965

July 21   Estimated cost: A£24,700,000 (A$49,400,000).

Aug 12   W.W. Wood writes confidential memo to Public Works Minister
          Davis Hughes in which he outlines measures to withhold
          Utzon's fees and the establishment of a drafting office.

Oct 27   Davis Hughes takes over responsibility for payments to Utzon.

1966

Feb 28   Utzon withdraws from the SOH project.

Apr 19   Utzon's replacements are announced.

Apr 28   Utzon flies out of Sydney.

Dec 12   Hall, Todd & Littlemore panel submit Review of Programme
          report which concludes a dual–purpose hall is unworkable.

1967

Sept 4   Estimated cost: A$85,000,000.

1973

Oct 20   Official opening of SOH by Queen Elizabeth II.

1974

May   Minister for Public Works announces that the final bill for SOH
          is A$102,000,000.

1978

June 20   Utzon receives Royal Institute of British Architects' Gold Medal.

1979

May   SOH organ completed at cost of A$1,200,000; original cost
          estimated at A$400,000.

1994

Nov 1   *Unseen Utzon* Exhibition.

1995

Oct 23   Premier Carr asks Utzon to serve as the principal consultant
          to the Sydney Opera House Trust.

2003

April   Utzon awarded Pritzker Prize.

To Jane, Rupert, Chantal, William, Sophie and Alice

INTRODUCTION

In April 2003 Jørn Utzon, at the age of 85, was awarded the Pritzker Prize – architecture's 'Nobel'. The citation reads: 'There is no doubt that the Sydney Opera House is his masterpiece. It is one of the great iconic buildings of the twentieth century, an image of great beauty which has become known throughout the world – a symbol for not only a city, but a whole country and continent'. The presentation of the prize places Utzon in the pantheon of the greatest contemporary architects but marks a career that failed to reach its full potential following the traumas of building the Opera House.

Since it opened in 1973 the Opera House has repaid its A$100 million cost many times over as a tourist attraction and as a cultural centre. As a brand it is priceless. The story of its construction is one of triumph and of tragedy; it is Utzon's masterpiece, yet he did not complete the building; the creation of the huge oversailing roofs was a magnificent feat of engineering and collaboration, but the design team split apart amidst misunderstandings and recriminations.

Today the building is loved, yet while it was under construction attitudes were very different. The local press continually attacked its cost, its delays and its architect; headline writers gave the now familiar white shell roofs nicknames such as 'the concrete camel', 'copulating terrapins' and 'the hunchback of Bennelong Point'. Politicians tried to control the costs and speed up the programme. In 1966, the pressures reached such a climax that Utzon wrote to Davis Hughes, then Minister for Public Works in the New South Wales Government, saying 'You have forced me to leave the job'. Hughes immediately accepted what he took to be the architect's resignation.

Soon after Utzon left, Davis Hughes hired three local architects, Peter Hall, Lionel Todd and David Littlemore, to complete the building which finally opened on 20 October 1973 – six years behind schedule and costing more than ten times its original estimate.

The significance of the Opera House is not merely in its iconic status. The building identified Utzon as a member of what Siegfried Giedeon called the 'Third Generation' of Modernist architects who sought a more plastic and more humane way of building. It buried the Modernist concept that 'form follows function' and led the way for landmark cultural buildings. According to Frank Gehry: 'without his [Utzon's] vision, there would hardly be the Guggenheim in Bilbao today'. Utzon's desire to push the boundaries of architecture wherever he could meant that the building became a test bed for new technologies in construction. His interest in the use of repetitive elements – what he called 'Additive Architecture' – arising from the prefabrication of sections of the Sydney roof shells, was in the forefront of thinking about the manufacture of buildings. The use of computers for structural design was in its infancy, but the roof shells could not have been done without them. Computers were also used for the first time in the positioning of elements of the roof during construction. The use of epoxy resins for jointing precast concrete, sealants, laminated glass and planar glazing had never been attempted before on such a scale. The Opera House story also raised questions about the need for changes in the management of major contracts, and advanced considerably the concept of project management in the construction industry.

These successes were garnered from a project which stretched many of those involved to the limit, professionally, personally and psychologically. The seeds of the tensions that surrounded the Opera House project were sown right at the start by the decision to use a single stage open competition to choose the architect.

This method of selection has, over the past 150 years, produced some great pieces of architecture, but has regularly been the centre of scandal, argument and failure. The competitions for the Crystal Palace (1851), Paris Opera (1861), the Law Courts in the Strand (1868), the Paris Opera de la Bastille (1989), the Bibliothèque Nationale de Paris (1993) and the Cardiff Opera House (1994) all became embroiled in arguments between the participants whether they were politicians, jurors, clients or disgruntled losers.

In open competitions the architects' submissions are anonymous. The jurors select the winning scheme on the basis of a prescribed set of drawings with little idea of the entrant's experience or abilities. Their decision is based on the architectural quality and the excitement of the submitted drawings, and they are frequently looking for a scheme that will be important architecturally. When the Sydney Opera House jurors found what they were looking for, they announced 'This has the opportunity of being one of the world's great buildings.'

While the competition system does have the advantage of discovering new talent it runs the risk of selecting a scheme that the client does not really want, an architect who can design but cannot build and a building that does not work. The judging process throws up designs that are visually and architectural striking – and often ignores the more reticent entries.

The system also demands a huge number of unpaid man-hours on the part of the architect. Despite this, many architectural practices are willing to expend the time, not just for the chance of winning, but to test their architectural ideas, to keep their eye in and to develop their staff.

As a direct result of the Sydney Opera House, open competitions have been used less and less with a growing preference for limited competitions where the organizers check architects' credentials before they invite them to participate.

Today, the influence of the architect in the building team is a fraction of what it was in the 1950s when he took on much of the management role of a project. He was unquestionably the leading professional in the team; the other members expected that the architect would control the programme and the production of drawings.

However, the Sydney Opera House project did not work like this.

When Utzon won the competition, Ove Arup and Partners were engaged as structural and civil engineers directly by the client, the NSW Government, rather than by the architect as was more normal in Australia at the time. Arups were also given responsibility for all the other engineering disciplines – electrical, heating and ventilating, acoustic and theatrical – which was thought to be a more convenient arrangement not unlike a civil engineering contract in which the engineer is the principal agent of the client and responsible for the administration and supervision of construction.

This contractual structure conflicted with Utzon's own view of the architect's pre-eminent role, and led to misunderstandings between Utzon and Arups in the later stages of the project.

But for the first stages Utzon and Arups worked harmoniously together. Ove Arup believed Utzon was the best architect he had ever worked with. In Denmark and London architects and engineers collaborated to create the great shells, the form of which was the result of a true marriage of their two disciplines. When both offices moved to Sydney and Utzon's attention turned to the interiors, the goodwill gradually evaporated and the process of collaborative design ceased.

It is remarkable that today, against so many odds, the Opera House stands proud against its Sydney Harbour backdrop. Its very existence is a tribute to political vision, to Utzon's genius, to Arup's structural expertise, the teams of engineers of all kinds, the contractors who made it happen and to Hall Todd and Littlemore. As Utzon told ABC Radio in an interview in 2002: 'Sometimes in architecture it happens that a daring step into the unknown gives us great gifts for the future.'

CHAPTER 1
A MAGNIFICENT DOODLE

In 1957, it took three days to fly from London Heathrow to Sydney and cost £430 and 4 shillings sterling. The journey included refuelling stops in Zurich, Istanbul, Karachi, Calcutta, Singapore, Jakarta and Darwin. Communication by telephone was expensive, connections had to be booked in advance and the quality of line was variable. Urgent communication was generally by telex or telegram. Today we inhabit a world of instant communications, of faxes, mobile phones, e-mails and the internet: it is hard to recall the meaning of distance in the days before the jet plane took over the skies. An appreciation of just how far away Sydney seemed from Europe in the 1950s is important in understanding the difficulties that beset the design and construction of the Opera House. The complications of cultural differences, of communications, of professional procedures and the fact that the long-distance traveller was virtually incommunicado all played their part in the unfolding drama.

It was clearly unrealistic for many of the overseas entrants to the Opera House competition to visit the proposed site and the first time Jørn Utzon saw the New South Wales capital and Bennelong Point, the striking promontory selected for the building, was in July 1957, six months after it was announced that he had won the competition for the new building. Utzon had studied the qualities of the promontory from photographs and postcards. It is a mark of his genius that he so brilliantly interpreted the location, the light and the landscape with his sculptural forms.

On first seeing Bennelong Point, he exclaimed to a *Sydney Morning Herald* reporter, 'It's absolutely breathtaking. There's no opera site in the world to compare with it ...this site is even more beautiful than in the photographs from which I worked.'

The selection of Bennelong Point for the future Sydney Opera House had been pinpointed in the early 1940s by the National Theatre Movement of Australia, but it was the support of Eugene Goossens, conductor of the Sydney Symphony Orchestra (SSO) that ensured its selection in preference to sites in the centre of town. Goossens was a driving force behind the project. He had been invited to take over the orchestra by Charles Moses, the General Manager of the Australian Broadcasting Commission (ABC). In order to match the salary Goossens was receiving at the time from the Cincinnatti Symphony Orchestra, Moses arranged for him to act as Director of the Sydney Conservatorium, which is located in the Royal Botanic Gardens overlooking Circular Quay and Bennelong Point.

At that time, SSO concerts were given in the Sydney Town Hall. Although acoustically adequate, it was hardly a suitable venue for Australia's top orchestra. It also lacked basic facilities; it was virtually unheatable in winter and concert-goers were forced to don hats and gloves. The Sydney Town Hall management refused to provide any sort of refreshments and the audience had to decamp to the pub across the road at the interval. Many of the regular concert-goers were recent immigrants from Europe where they were used to much better facilities.

The SSO programme of concerts was well established; opera, however, was a minority interest. There were some local amateur groups and the occasional tour from an Italian company, but that was it. As a city, Sydney was overshadowed by Melbourne and was a far cry from the cosmopolitan metropolis it is today. It was something of a backwater where the pubs closed at 6.00pm.

Goossens arrived to take up his post in July 1947 and told the *Sydney Morning Herald* that he would build up the SSO into one of the six best orchestras in the world; he wanted to create a fine concert hall with perfect acoustics and seating for 3,500 people, a home for an opera company and a smaller hall for chamber music. The brief for the Sydney Opera House was born.

Goossens plugged away for several years with little official response to his idea until 1954 when, through Moses' good offices, he met the Labor Premier, Joe Cahill, to explain his plans. The response was positive. The decision to hold the 1956 Olympic Games in Melbourne had prompted Sydney to try and raise its sights and a cultural initiative of this kind was just what was needed. Cahill agreed to call a public meeting to discuss the 'question of the establishment of an opera house in Sydney.' The meeting was held in the

The Fort Macquarie Tram Depot, completed in 1902, which previously occupied the Opera House site.

Sydney Public Library on 20 November of that year and was attended by several hundred people involved in the world of music, theatre and dance as well as civic and business leaders.

At the meeting, Cahill proposed that a committee be set up comprising Eugene Goossens, Henry Ingham Ashworth, Professor of Architecture at the University of Sydney, Charles Moses and Stan Haviland, Under Secretary at the Department of Local Government.

Describing his dream for an opera house, Goossens compared it to the San Francisco Opera House, which provided for orchestra, opera, ballet and choral festival in an all-purpose building. Since Goossens had taken over the SSO, the demand for symphonic concerts had more than doubled, necessitating an increasing number of repeat performances; a larger hall accommodating a bigger audience would cut down on these, freeing up the orchestra to support an additional opera programme. He then explained his thinking as to the size of halls – a critical element of the brief and one of the major problems that was to face Utzon some ten years later:

'At orchestra and choral concerts 3,500 to 4,000 can listen adequately and comfortably. Grand opera is best presented to audiences of 1,800 to 2,500, though theatres in Milan and elsewhere have larger audiences. In my own former town of Cincinnatti, operatic performances are given in buildings accommodating 3,800 patrons. The effective presentation of drama involves much smaller audiences – 1,500–1,800.'

He described Malmö Opera House in Sweden, which has a capacity of 1,800 but with the use of travelling walls could be converted into a theatre with 1,200 seats or a hall for recitals with 800:

'The right approach would be to envisage an auditorium large enough to seat from 3,500 to 4,000 people and to make the auditorium adaptable, by simple mechanism, for opera, for drama and other users, for which a smaller auditorium is desirable.'

Goossens confirmed his view that Bennelong Point was the ideal site: 'Imagine visitors on a liner coming up Sydney Harbour, seeing this magnificent building and being told "That is Sydney's opera house".' In addition, it was conveniently close to the Sydney Conservatorium and it made sense that his two places of work were close to each other.

At the time, the site housed Sydney's main tram depot, which the Department of Transport was none too keen to move. They were overridden by Cahill, however, who announced on 17 May 1955 that the new Opera House would be on Bennelong Point, which would provide a setting 'unique

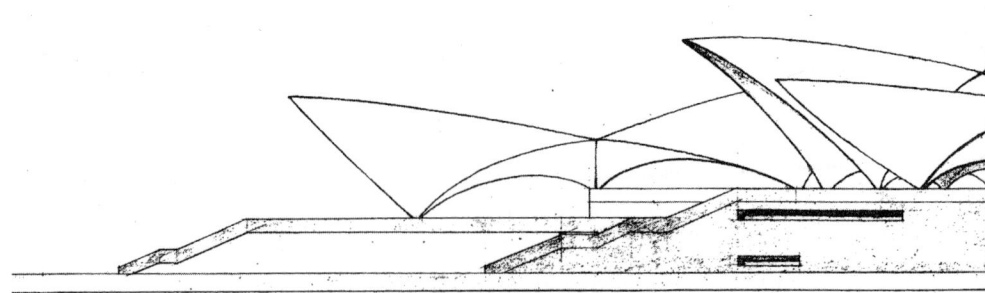

The competition winning design, its form more free-flowing and organic than the completed building.

in the world for a building of such monumental character as an opera house'.

It was accepted that there should be a competition for the new building, although there was some debate as to whether this should be open to architects internationally or only to Australian practitioners. The NSW Chapter of the Royal Australian Institute of Architects (RAIA) suggested, unsurprisingly, that it should be open to nationals only. In this, the Chapter was supported by Walter Bunning, a leading Sydney architect who many expected to win the competition and who was to become a regular critic of Utzon's designs.

The Sydney Opera House Executive Committee (SOHEC) opted for an international open competition in the hope of attracting the best talent in the world. It was perhaps understandable that it had little sympathy for the local architects' position: Goossens was born in England and had had an extensive international career; Moses was born in England, emigrating to Australia in the 1920s; Ashworth, also from England, had only arrived in Sydney in 1949 having served in the army in India. His batman accompanied him from England; students of the time recall the batman operating the slide machine for Ashworth's lectures. It was agreed that the judges should be Leslie Martin, then chief architect of the London County Council and architect of the Royal Festival Hall in London, and Eero Saarinen, architect of a number of major buildings in America including the Kresge Auditorium on the

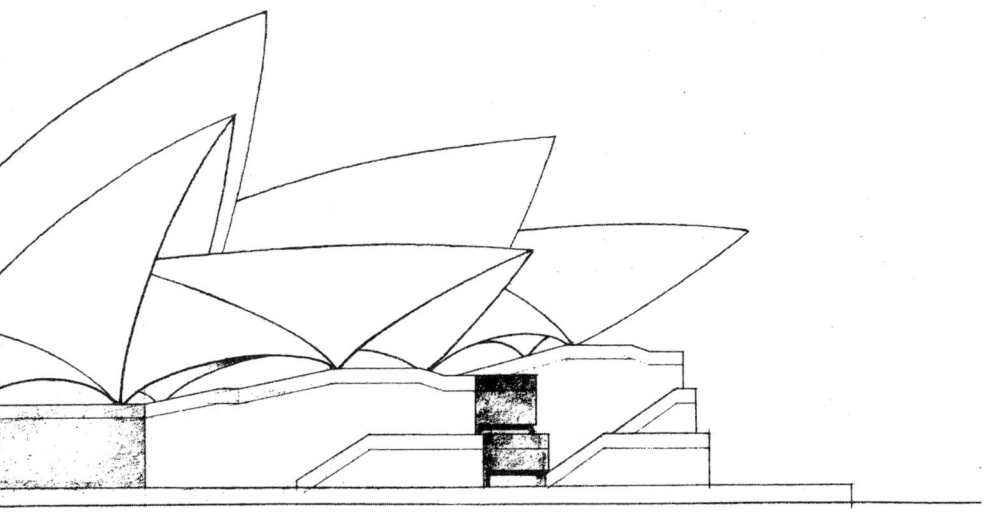

Massachusetts Institute of Technology Campus and the TWA terminal at Idlewild (later Kennedy) Airport. Both these buildings used thin concrete shell roofs. Saarinen was working on the design of the TWA building at the time of the Sydney competition. The other judges were the Australian-born Cobden Parkes, the NSW Government Architect, and Professor Ashworth.

Disaster struck on 9 March 1956 when Goossens, who had been knighted the year before, was arrested at Sydney Airport after he was found in possession of 1,100 'indecent items' including photographs and rubber masks. He resigned from his posts and left Australia two weeks later. The Opera House project had not only lost a great champion, but SOHEC also lost a member who had a comprehensive understanding of the requirements of the brief and the practical experience of using the most sophisticated concert halls around the world.

The winner of the competition was to receive A£5,000, second prize was A£2,000 and third A£1,000 (at the time there was a fixed rate of exchange A£1.25 : £1 sterling); no costs were stated although the brief suggested that 'extravagance cannot be entertained'. The building requirements stated that the winning scheme was unlikely to be built without changes, so they were looking for a 'sound basic scheme by a competent architect'.

The detailed brief asked for a building enclosing two halls; the larger one to seat between 3,000 and 3,500 people, the smaller one to hold approximately 1,200. The functions of each hall were set out in order of priority:

Large Hall (Major Hall)
1. Symphony concerts (including organ music and soloists)
2. Large scale opera
3. Ballet and dance
4. Choral
5. Pageants and mass meetings

Small Hall (Minor Hall)
1. Dramatic presentations
2. Intimate opera
3. Chamber music
4. Concerts and recitals
5. Lectures

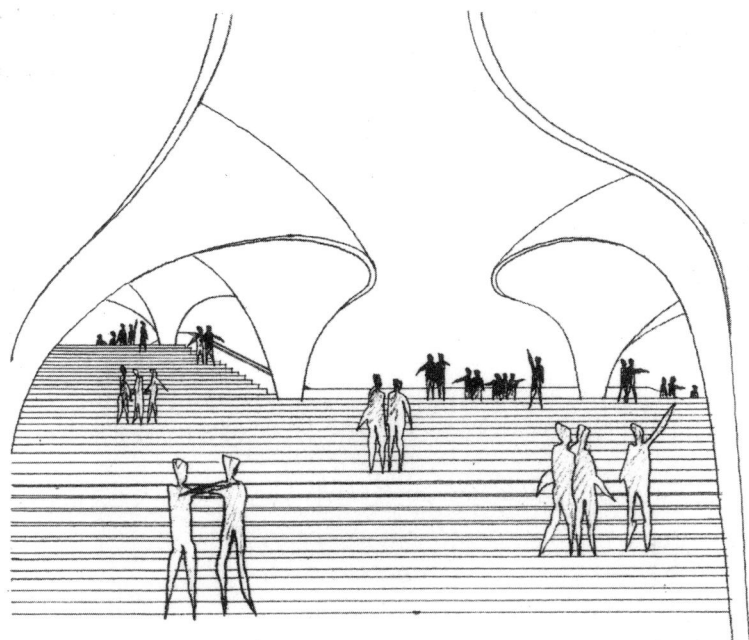

Perspective from main entrance.

The order of priorities is significant in light of the difficulties Utzon had in accommodating the requirements of the brief and of the decision by Hall Todd and Littlemore, the architectural team that took over after Utzon resigned, to drop opera from the Major Hall.

When the competition closed, there were 217 entries from 27 countries, including 61 from Australia and 53 from the UK. On 29 January at the Art Gallery of New South Wales, the Premier, Joe Cahill, announced that Jørn Utzon of Hellebæk, Denmark was the winner.

Much of the interest in Utzon's building has focused on the dramatic form of the roofs, but there were other striking and radical features to his design. Unlike all the other entrants, he placed the two theatres side by side, but only managed to do so by ignoring the competition rules; the other entries placed the theatres end to end.

Utzon's solution had the advantage that the entrance to each hall is equally accessible from the south, the city side. Based on the classical principles of the Greek amphitheatre, he sat the auditoria on the raking podium – a massive plinth which reflected Utzon's admiration for the Mayan

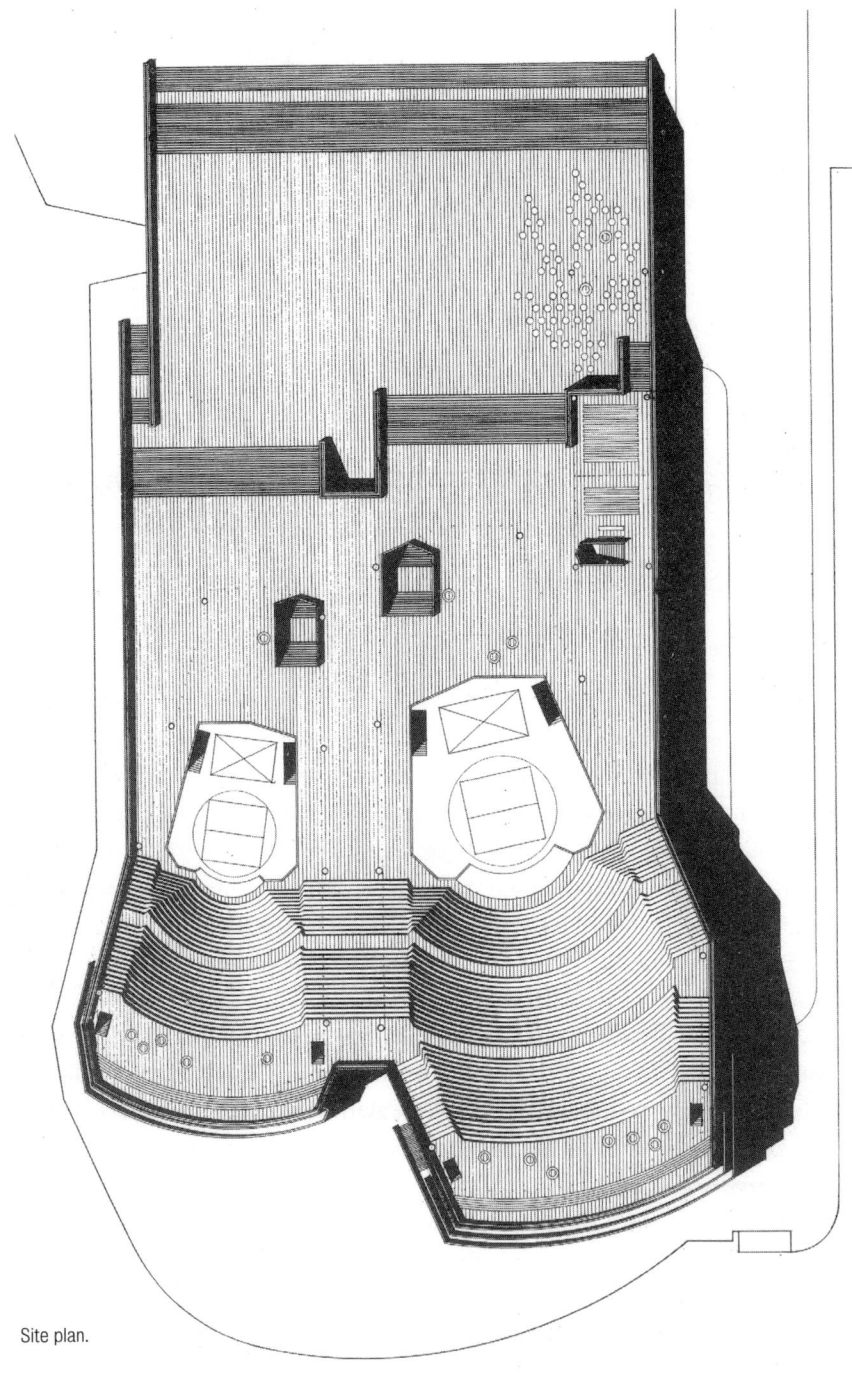

Site plan.

The highly commended entry by John Clark and Ian Plenderleath was typical of the orthogonal architecture of many of the entries with the two halls placed end to end, rather than side by side as Utzon did.

architecture of Mesoamerica – where the floor levels inside were matched by those on the outside. This meant that at every level there was easy egress thus, at a stroke, solving one of the major problems of large public buildings – escape in the case of fire. This brilliant and elegant solution eliminated the need for space-consuming escape stairs that would otherwise be required and was simultaneously economical and safe. However, access to the seats from the entrance foyer required passing on either side of the stage area, which meant Utzon could only provide limited wing space rather than the usual side stages. Apart from providing space for a waiting chorus in grand opera and ballet, the side stages play an essential part in most theatres for scene-changing. Utzon proposed instead a series of lifts that would shift scenery vertically from the service areas below the stage. The stage machinery would be enclosed within the podium along with all the non-public areas, service facilities and an experimental theatre.

If the assessors had enforced the competition conditions, Utzon's proposals would have been disqualified. He had not included the required drawings, he presented enlarged sketches and no perspective drawing. His presentation was described by the Australian art critic Robert Hughes as 'nothing more than a magnificent doodle'. But a doodle that illustrated not just the cleverness of the plan but also the iconic potential of the forms. That this powerful image, abstract yet subject to interpretation as clouds, billowing sails, nun's cowls or mating turtles, can be so simply drawn explains the global impact of the design – its profile converting easily to logotypes, t-shirts, guide book covers and souvenir gewgaws.

The site requirements stated that, 'the building may be located anywhere on the site, but should not be placed right on the boundary', and that an entry would be disqualified if 'it exceeds the limit of the site as outlined on the site plan'. Utzon's scheme exceeded the site boundaries to the west.

The brief asked for 3,000 to 3,500 seats in the Major Hall, as Goossens had recommended. Utzon's proposals could not accommodate these numbers. The client later reduced the requirement to 2,800, but this too turned out to be unachievable.

The cavalier attitude of the assessors to the rules of the competition caused much chagrin among the unsuccessful competitors, but more importantly the width of the site was to prove critical in the years to come as Utzon struggled to squeeze sufficient accommodation onto the site.

Paul Boissevain, of Boissevain and Osmond, who won third prize had experience of concert halls prior to entering the competition. They worked with theatre consultants and acousticians for six months to produce their entry and Boissevain realized immediately when he saw Utzon's plan the problems there would be fitting in all the required accommodation. 'It was a brilliant conception, but fatally flawed.'

Martin and Saarinen had lunch with the English architect, Trevor Dannatt, shortly after the judging where Saarinen made it quite clear that both he and Martin had lighted on the Utzon design as being in an entirely different league from the rest of the competitors.

The assessors' report said, 'We consider this scheme to be the most original and creative submission… The white sail-like forms of the shell vaults relate as naturally to the harbour as the sails of its yachts.' In defence of the judges' decision, Ashworth told the *Sun Herald*, 'I was surprised there were not more schemes of a more advanced character in terms of architectural thinking. I imagined we'd be spoilt for choice with half a dozen outstanding designs; instead there was only one.'

Saarinen, with his experience of concrete shell structures, had been a strong supporter of the design. During the judging he had even sketched the perspectives that Utzon had omitted in order to illustrate its architectural qualities. When it came to putting a figure to the costs of the sails, Saarinen advised the quantity surveyor from the local firm of Rider Hunt and Partners as there were no examples of similar shell structures in Australia on which to base the calculations. 'There's nothing to it,' said Saarinen. 'The shells might be about three inches thick at the top, and say 12 inches thick at the base.'

From these figures, the quantity surveyor was able to calculate the likely cost of the Utzon entry as A£3.6million. The assessors were pleased to note that, of the placed schemes, Utzon's was the most economical.

As might be expected of any project of this kind, reactions were mixed. Ashworth believed that local criticisms were directed as much to the expenditure related to a project of this kind as to the architecture itself. Local architect Harry Seidler, who was himself one of the unsuccessful entrants to the competition, was supportive and remains one of Utzon's most stalwart defenders to this day. In 1957, he wrote to the *Sydney Morning Herald*:

'Architecture is a language and architects speak it. Most of them just barely manage to speak – very few ever speak eloquent prose, but it happens rarely indeed that any of them create poetry with just a few words.'

'Our proposed Opera House is just such poetry, spoken with exquisite economy of words. But then how many of us appreciate or even understand poetry when we have only ever heard crude language.'

In contrast, Walter Bunning described the design as 'an insect with a shell on its back which has crawled out from under a log'.

From further afield, the doyen of American architecture, 89-year-old Frank Lloyd Wright, a major influence on Utzon, was equally forthright: 'This circus tent is not architecture.' Functionalist modernists hated the building. When Utzon went to visit Mies van der Rohe in America, the architect of the Lake Shore Drive apartments and the Seagram Building refused to see him.

Central to the local debate was – and remained throughout the life of the project – the subject of cost. Such debate is inevitable in major public projects. Members of Cahill's Labor Party felt unhappy about the expenditure in light of a crisis in school building and a shortage of 150,000 homes. There were estimated to be some 250,000 men, women and children living 'in huts, sheds and sharing inadequate housing'. It was clear that Cahill would be unable to convince his party that the Opera House should be paid for out of public funds.

It was not until 4 July 1958 that the Labor Caucus agreed to go ahead with the project after Cahill assured them that the Government would contribute no more than A£100,000. The Lord Mayor of Sydney was to be invited to open an appeal for funds. The possibility of launching lotteries to finance the scheme would be addressed after the public appeal had opened.

'The political battle has now been won,' Ashworth wrote to Martin in London, and he invited Utzon to come to Sydney for the first time.

Meanwhile, in Europe, Martin and Saarinen had met with Utzon. They were conscious that the Dane had had little experience of building larger projects and felt that he needed assistance. It is not unusual in competitions which have been won by architects who do not have the background or resources to complete a large-scale project to be teamed up with a larger firm – nicknamed 'uncles' – to ensure the smooth running of the job. Cobden Parks, the Government Architect, was insistent that Utzon should work with a local architect. Utzon rejected this proposal. After discussions with Utzon, Martin and Saarinen announced that they were convinced that he did not require further architectural support. 'He is admirably equipped to deal with all matters of design.'

However, he did require assistance in the problems of calculating and building the complicated shell vault system, and it was proposed that he should receive technical support from an engineering company, such as Ove Arup and Partners in London who had recently completed the Brynmawr Factory in Wales using 3in (8cm) thick, 82ft x 62ft (25m x 19m) shell roofs, or Christiani and Nielsen in Copenhagen, a Danish company with significant experience in reinforced concrete design and construction. 'We feel that this collaboration would give Utzon any support which he might need on the managerial and financial side of the work.'

However, Arup had already written to Utzon offering his firm's services: 'Congratulations on the first prize! I am very glad that it was a Dane that won and after seeing a sketch of your project, I am even happier – and not a little surprised – that such a fanciful but unusual project has been chosen instead of just being praised as is usually the case.

'So far as I can see, it would not be easy to calculate and detail your plans so as to give justice to your ideas with full clarity and still make them economically possible. Nor do I believe you can count on Australian workmen and Australian technical resources being on the same level as the Danish.

'If my firm can be of assistance to you in any way, it would give me great pleasure. I have of course over 30 years' experience in co-operating with English architects and institutions and my partner Mr Jenkins is probably the leading authority in the structural field.'

It has been suggested by the Australian architectural writer, Philip Drew, that the Italian engineer/architect Pier Luigi Nervi might have been a better choice of engineer. Nervi had designed and built a number of large concrete structures, including a massive 310ft (94.5m) span exhibition hall in Turin, and in 1957 was designing the concrete dome for the Palazzo dello Sport in Rome. Nervi, however, was scornful of the Sydney proposals. Nor was Utzon particularly keen on the look of Nervi's structures; he told Yuzo Mikami, who worked in his office from 1958 to 1961 before moving to Arups, 'Nervi likes to design everything with rib or lamella like things crisscrossing under the roof. I didn't want that sort of thing. I wanted to see a smooth concave surface like the inside of an egg.' The Mexican architect and builder, Felix Candela, another concrete shell specialist, was unimpressed by the competition drawings. On seeing the winning design he remarked, 'These shells are not self supporting.' When the shells were completed in 1967, he said, 'The Sydney Opera House is a tragic example of the catastrophic consequences of this attitude of disdain for the most obvious laws of physics.'

Professor Henry J Cowan, Professor of Architectural Science at the University of Sydney, explains the structural problems raised by Utzon's design: 'If you take an egg as an example of a shell structure, it is able in its complete state to support a load of up to 70kg. If you cut the egg in half its strength is reduced to a fraction of the integral form. Cut it in quarters and it has no strength at all.' Essentially the Sydney Opera House design is made up of a series of quarter shells. Astonishingly, when Utzon was preparing his competition entry he took no engineering advice.

Ashworth wrote to Utzon in February stating his preference for Ove Arup and Partners, and in March Utzon agreed to work with the engineers who were based in the Fitzrovia area of London.

With the selection of the dramatis personae, the stage was set for the action to commence. The leading players were all Danes – Utzon, Arup (although a British national) and Vilhelm Jordan, Utzon's acoustics consultant.

Jørn Utzon was 38 in 1957. He was born in Copenhagen where his father was a naval architect. He enrolled at the Kunstakademiet in Copenhagen in 1937 to study architecture, completing his degree in 1942 before leaving occupied Denmark for neutral Sweden where he

Jørn Utzon

Ove Arup

joined the Danish Brigade resistance group while working for a number of different architectural practices.

By the time he won the competition, Utzon had completed a scheme of 21 terraced houses and designed the Kingo Housing complex, a series of 64 courtyard houses linked in groups and laid like an elegant necklace across the landscape, reflecting his understanding of context and his fascination with repetitive elements. These were constructed between 1957 and 1960. There is little in the design of this modern vernacular *parti* that presages the full-blooded plasticity of his Opera House entry.

Utzon's approach to the design for the Opera House was clearly enhanced by his close relationship with the sea. His home and studio at Hellebæk overlooked the Oresund, the strip of water that separates Denmark and Sweden, and he was a keen sailor. He frequently referred to the castle at Elsinore, which is visible from Hellebæk, as one of his inspirations for the Opera House design.

His architectural masters were Aalto and Asplund. He admired the fact that Aalto 'never worked in plan, he always worked in spaces'. In 1966, after

Utzon resigned from the Opera House, Siegfried Giedion, the author of *Space, Time and Architecture*, published an additional chapter to his seminal book in the magazine *Zodiac*. He placed Utzon among the 'Third Generation' of modernist architects. This group had certain recognizable elements that differentiated them from the generation of Mies van der Rohe, Gropius and Le Corbusier, of which the most apparent was 'the right of expression above pure function.'

Utzon was tall, handsome and charming. He was good and exhilarating company. When he arrived in Sydney he was treated like a film star – and looked like one. He was a superb presenter and adept at convincing his clients of the benefits of his ideas.

Ove Arup was born on 16 April 1895 in Newcastle-upon-Tyne, son of a Danish veterinary surgeon father and a Norwegian mother. Educated in Denmark, he entered Copenhagen University in 1913 to study philosophy and mathematics, but in 1916 he switched to engineering. After graduating he joined the firm of Christiani and Nielsen in Hamburg before moving to London in 1923.

In the early 1930s he met the architect Berthold Lubetkin, who was looking for a way of building the cylindrical concrete drum for the Gorilla House at London Zoo. The resulting collaborative partnership of engineer and architect, where the roles were so integrated that apportionment of authorship is impossible, was a formative influence on the young Arup; it conditioned his own professional development and that of the company he was to found. Of Lubetkin, he said, '…for him architecture was a battle to be won with every means at his disposal. He… taught me that "sensible building" must be modified to satisfy the claims of aesthetics.'

Lubetkin was a beaux arts-trained architect who, like Utzon, was a critic of Modernism's hygienic anonymity. The work of Tecton, the practice founded by Lubetkin, delighted in the plasticity of concrete, and the spiral ramp of the Penguin Pool at London Zoo – designed with Arup – is one of the most poetic examples of the marriage of architecture and engineering.

In 1933, Arup joined J L Kier and Company (a Danish company, the name is the anglicized form of Kjaer) who were doing pioneering work in reinforced structures. He joined the firm as chief designer and director on condition that they would carry out building projects. This allowed him to build a series of residential blocks with Tecton, including Highpoint 1 and Highpoint 2, both important landmarks in the development of Modernism in

Britain in the 1930s. In 1938 he formed the construction company of Arup and Arup, with his cousin Arne Arup, and during the war worked on the development of concrete air-raid shelters and the construction of the Mulberry Harbours used in the Normandy landings in 1945.

In 1946, he set up Ove Arup and Partners providing structural engineering advice to the architectural profession. By the time of the Sydney competition, the firm had built up a considerable reputation among architects, although it was still viewed by the engineering establishment as a maverick firm; Arup was always a rebel and outsider. Peter Rice, who was to become a leading light in the firm, said, 'I had joined Ove Arup and Partners because I had heard it was a place where an oddball could fit in... Ove Arup defined an attitude – an integrity towards what one did that permeated down from his remote and distant 6th floor office.'

At one stage, the engineer Sir Frederick Snow attempted to blackball Arup from the Association of Consulting Engineers because he had been running a contracting company – such links with 'trade' were anathema to the professionals of the period.

Arup was a complex mixture of other-worldliness and pragmatism. His early education in philosophy gave him a lifelong enthusiasm for the bigger picture and an undogmatic interest in ideas. He was not materialistic and had little interest in the financial aspects of running the practice. His personal assistant, Ruth Winaver, remembered him emerging from a meeting with the formidable Miss Mant, who looked after the Arup office accounts in the 1950s. Miss Mant wanted to settle some financial queries. After the meeting, Arup wandered out of his office and said, 'I've been listening to Miss Mant for a good half hour and I haven't any idea what she was talking about.'

In an interview with Peter Rawsthorne in 1965 he said, 'It has always amazed me that people want to go on all their lives just making more and more money. To be a business man with the idea of making money always seemed to me to be absurd. It just goes round in a circle. You make money in order to live and you live in order to make money. There doesn't seem to be any idea behind that.'

He would talk at great length on topics that interested him, words often tumbling out and over each other in sentences that, taken individually, seemed to make little sense, but when seen within the context of the whole were utterly convincing. Although he was in his sixties during the design and construction of the Opera House, he retained a boundless enthusiasm and a youthful approach to life and to his work. Jack Zunz, the Arups engineer who played a major role in the Opera House saga, wrote in Arup's obituary: 'Like many great men, he was full of contradictions. He did not suffer fools gladly, yet was kindly and had no delusions of grandeur.'

Arup was a perfectionist and would go to great lengths to get the right solution. In this, he and Utzon had much in common. Peter Dunican, who had joined Arup in 1943 and played a major part in building up the practice, wrote in 1965: 'Ove is a perfectionist with an absolute willingness to go back to the beginning and start again. It can be a tiresome trait and sometimes very upsetting [for those who have] made all the drawings that are being torn up.' It was a trait that certainly upset the engineers of the first shell scheme for the Opera House when, after three years' work, Arup decided to pursue an alternative route.

But he was also a very practical builder. His experience with Christiani and Nielsen and with Kier had given him a clear understanding of how structures were built, in particular the nature of concrete formwork and the essential need for the repetition of elements.

When Arup started working with Utzon, he appeared to be the architect that Arup had been waiting for all his professional life. Importantly, along with his charm and his obvious design skills, he was Danish.

One of Arup's driving philosophies was that of 'total architecture', which he defined as the implication that 'all relevant design decisions have been considered together and have been integrated into a whole by a well organized team empowered to fix priorities.' By example, and by his writing he – probably more than anyone else – halted the divergence between architecture and engineering that began in the nineteenth century. The relationship between the architect and the engineer is at the heart of the Opera House story. The nature of the competition-winning design ensured that this was the case.

The traditional way for architects to employ their engineers' advice was to design the building and then ask the engineer to make sure it would stand up. This might require some adaptation of the shape of the building and size of the structural members, but the engineer's brief would be to retain the scale, proportions and quality of the architect's original design. Such an approach worked well when architecture largely consisted of beams, columns and walls, but as architectural designs became more complex and new technology allowed previously unknown freedom of form and size, the engineer joined the design process at an earlier stage. Instead of being handed finished designs and imposing a solution, the engineer became part of the design team.

In the case of the Opera House, the design of the building had been carried out and was fixed in the public consciousness before any engineer became involved. Arups had little choice but to try and make the competition entry work. At their first interview, Arup told Utzon that the shape of the shells was not very suitable structurally. 'It soon became clear,' according to Arup, 'that any alteration to the cross section would completely destroy the architectural character. So in the end Utzon and I decided that the scheme had to go ahead as designed by Utzon, more or less…'.

Writing to SOHEC in July 1957, Arup raised the point that the shells were all different in shape and therefore did not permit the repetition of elements as is normal in reinforced concrete work. Without being able to repeat the pieces, new shuttering would have to be made for each section, thus increasing costs and time. Utzon had already proposed covering the roof with tiles; once the shells were built this would entail individually laying millions of tiles by hand. It was clear to the engineers that some form of repetitive geometry was essential if the building was ever to get off the drawing board.

While a substantial number of buildings around the world had been built using single-curve concrete shell techniques, the technology of double-curved structures such as the Opera House was still in its infancy. To reassure reporters of the durability of such designs, when he arrived in Sydney in July 1957 Utzon told them, 'In Berlin recently, I saw a congress hall with such a roof spanning about 240ft [73m], and it was only three inches thick.' With hindsight, he could not have made a worse comparison. In May 1980, the roof of the Berlin building collapsed burying a journalist under the debris – a reminder of the dangers inherent in building and the requirement for all those involved to ensure that life is not put at risk. When new designs are pushing at the edges of the possible these responsibilities become all the greater.

Utzon took a model of the Opera House design with him to Sydney; the model still reflected the competition entry with freeform shells and a lower profile than the one we now recognize. It is likely that, just as Utzon had not sought any engineering advice for his designs, nor had he consulted experts on theatre design. The heights allowed for stage machinery were clearly inadequate in the competition scheme, however, the section, which was now based on a parabola, provided more vertical space than the earlier shells and the problem was solved – for the time being at least.

While in Sydney, Utzon helped to launch the public appeal for money for the Opera House and, soon after, the formation of the lottery was announced. It was expected that at least two-thirds of the funds required would be in hand by the time the Opera House was finished and that the lottery would continue until all of the A£3.6million had been raised. On his departure, Utzon promised to return in six months' time with a first set of drawings and would prepare final technical drawings by February 1959.

True to his promise, Utzon returned to Sydney in March 1958 to present the developments of his design, which were published in an elegant document described as the 'Red Book' because of its striking red cover featuring the distinctive white profile of the Opera House shells cut roughly from a sheet of paper by Utzon himself. The report was jointly prepared with the other consultants – OAP, engineering, V L Jordan, acoustics, J Varming, mechanical services, M Balslev, electrical engineering and S Malmquist, theatre techniques. 'Through this [the Red Book] the outsider gets a glimpse into the mosaic of contemporary teamwork', wrote Giedion in Zodiac. In fact, it is something of a patchwork. Each consultant prepared their own section and it is clear that Utzon had yet to bring their individual contributions into a coherent design.

The cross section of the building shown in the book had begun to take the shape of the final design, with three shells on each hall facing north and the entrance shell facing south. The auditoria, however, are shown as simple rectangular sections, which reflect Jordan's views on the 'shoe box' hall being the most efficient acoustic space but have little of Utzon's hand in their design.

The shells have a more geometric and less free-form profile than the competition entry. Each shell consists of two symmetrical halves meeting in a ridge, the surfaces created by a series of coaxial parabolas. 'By defining the surfaces geometrically, each point of the surfaces can be given spatial co-ordinates,' wrote Arup in the Red Book, 'and a basis has been created for the calculation of the forces acting on the shells.' Without being able to define the structures mathematically, the engineers would have been unable to apply the laws of physics that underlie all their work.

Jordan set out the basis for his acoustic calculations for the Major Hall, which would hold 2,800 people for symphony concerts and would be converted for grand opera with an audience of 1,800 using movable platforms. 'Satisfactory acoustics,' Jordan wrote, 'are based on a number of factors: reverberation time, sound distribution, sound diffusion and the overall dimensions.' Reverberation time (RT) is, in simple terms, the time it takes for sound to bounce around a room before being absorbed by the materials and air; for concerts, Jordan suggested it should be 1.8–2.0 seconds, while 1.6–1.8 seconds was preferred for grand opera. Reverberation time became a major factor in the later stages of the project when Utzon was attempting to fit the required number of seats into the Major Hall. It is calculated with a formula developed by Wallace Clement Sabine at Harvard at the end of the nineteenth century and is based on the relationship between the air volume of the room and the total power of absorption of the room. To lengthen the RT the air volume must be increased or the power of absorption must be decreased, and vice versa. Since 60–70 per cent of total absorption in a hall is provided by the audience, it is clear that the volume provided per seat is critical. For concert halls, 350 cu ft (10 cu m) for each seat is generally accepted as appropriate, and almost twice that for opera which requires a shorter RT.

In the late 1950s, acoustic design was still in its infancy and Jordan was one of the early leaders in the field. He tested designs with the use of 1:10 models – the Opera House one was 30ft (9m) wide and 12ft (3.6m) high – using tape recordings of music speeded up in proportion to the scale of the model.

Like many aspects of design of the Opera House, the stage machinery was to break away from established methods, largely because of the lack of side stages. According to Malmquist, ' …we have broken out of the sterile shell of the baroque theatre and have discovered so many more ways to play theatre.'

The cost of the designs illustrated in the Red Book were calculated by quantity surveyors, Rider Hunt, to be A£4,781,200.

Utzon and Arup had a meeting with Joe Cahill who was insistent that work started in February 1959. Cahill was a Labor politician of the old school. He had been an aggressive and able trade union leader and had a reputation as a redneck, but he wanted to go down in history as a man of culture. An election was due in March 1959 and he recognized that, should the Liberal Party win, it could mean the end of the Opera House project. In addition, Cahill was not a well man, so he wanted Utzon and Arup to get on with it. Like Gilgamesh, King of Uruk, he believed in architecture as the key to immortality.

In order to allow for an early start it was decided to divide the job into three stages; Stage 1 would be the podium, Stage 2 the shells and Stage 3 the interiors and the windows.

Such fast-track construction makes sense for a design where the overall solution has been fixed; but for a design which is continually changing, it is hopeless. Thus the basic floor plan of the Opera House had to be fixed before the roof had been fully designed, leading to expensive alterations later on, and before Utzon had worked out how to fit in the required number of seats.

CHAPTER 2
COLLABORATION AND CREATIVITY

On his return journey from Sydney in March and April 1958, Utzon stopped off to visit China, Japan and Nepal, despite the enormous amount of work to be done on the podium. This was the first of a series of absences by Utzon at critical junctures in the programme. Later, when he moved to Australia, he closed his office down for three months and went travelling. Arups were unable to contact him and were forced to make a number of design decisions without Utzon's input. This was to have a significant effect on Utzon's relationship with his engineers.

However, in 1958 Ove Arup was still able to treat such incidents light-heartedly. When Utzon returned to Hellebæk, he wrote, 'It was nice to hear from you. I really thought you were lost in the wilds of Asia.'

For the next four years, the two men – and their teams – enjoyed a collaboration that was remarkable in its fruitfulness and, despite many traumas, was seen by most of those involved as a high point of architect/engineer collaboration.

The partner responsible for the project was Ronald Jenkins, although Arup, because of his Danish connections, was closely involved in the development of the designs.

Jenkins – whose initials, felicitously for an engineer, were RSJ – was a brilliant mathematician. Shy and socially diffident, he provided the hard detail that supported Arup's broadbrush philosophical approach. When Arup set up his firm of consulting engineers in 1946, Jenkins joined him becoming a senior partner in 1949. His major projects prior to the Opera House were the Brynmawr Rubber Company Factory, Hunstanton School – the seminal brutalist building by Alison and Peter Smithson – and a timber, hyperbolic paraboloid roof at Market Drayton. Peter Rice described him as 'an engineer whose mathematical elegance and precision made a great impression on me. He represented a kind of ideal, an engineer who combined mathematical rigour with a clear structural understanding of how things worked.'

On the Opera House, Jenkins was assisted by two Danes; Povl Ahm on the podium and Hugo Mollman on the shells. The Arups team enjoyed their trips to Hellebæk, its marvellous setting and its relaxed but hard-working and creative atmosphere made a refreshing change from the hurly burly of Fitzroy Street. The English architect, James Thomas, who worked at Hellebæk in 1960, described the studio as, 'An ivory tower to end all ivory towers.' There was only one telephone, no trade representatives were allowed in and there was no trade literature – Utzon would not accept ready-made solutions of any kind.

Working in the office had a timeless quality about it; Utzon was continually investigating new solutions but, with a reluctance to commit himself, he would worry away at a problem for months. When he was in Hellebæk, he would come in every day and go around the drawing-boards giving out sketches of his ideas for the architects to work on, or commenting on the development of solutions – the master with his small atelier of young disciples. While Thomas was in the office, the Australian architect, Os Jarvis, worked there for several months on documentation. Jarvis would tell Utzon that he should have a job architect whose priority was the Opera House. These comments annoyed Utzon who replied, 'I am the job architect.' There were rumours in the office that Jarvis was to set up the Utzon office in Sydney, but nothing came of it.

Utzon had a firm idea of his great abilities. Thomas describes Utzon as complex, confident, charming and patrician – 'but he could also be an absolute bugger.'

Rafael Moneo, the celebrated Spanish architect, arrived at the office in 1961 shortly after Thomas left. He had written to Utzon asking for a job, but received no reply, so he turned up on the doorstep and was accepted. Much of Moneo's year in Hellebæk was spent working on the spherical solution to the shells; he was responsible for many of the beautiful presentation drawings that explained the geometry.

The spirit of Arups' visits to Denmark is reflected in a letter Hugo Mollman wrote to Povl Ahm in 1959: 'No doubt you are enjoying life in Hellebæk, the "kolde bord" in the "badehotel" and bathing and sailing in Jørn's boats. Who knows you may even find some time for some work now and then.'

At that time, Yuzo Mikami was a key member of Utzon's office. He had been working for Junio Maekawa – one of Japan's leading architects who had worked with and been influenced by Le Corbusier – on the Japanese pavilion at Expo 1958 in Brussels. Mikami looked up to Utzon as a master, but he came from a different mould. He had a mathematical approach to his work; in keeping with his Japanese background, everything had to be very ordered. When Utzon asked him to design the Major Hall roof to reflect the beech forests around Hellebæk, his solution, designed while Utzon was away from the office, was a triangulated 'faceted' scheme that was very different to designs then being developed for the Minor Hall. Like Utzon, he was a perfectionist and an exquisite draftsman.

Arup's strong and personal relationship with Utzon meant that he was involved in many of the discussions but the day-to-day responsibility was in the hands of Jenkins who worked fairly independently on the shells. 'He was not the sort of person who liked to have someone breathing down his neck', according to Povl Ahm.

Stage 1, the podium, included the foundations and columns that would support the shell roofs above, the 900 rooms that service the halls and the entrance concourse area with pedestrian access above and car drop off below. At 600ft x 312ft (183m x 95m) rising to 83ft (25m) above sea level at the top seating level at the north end, it was, at the time, the largest concrete building in the southern hemisphere. At the south end, folded slab beams span 161ft (49m) across the concourse. These sculptured ribs form a striking introduction to the Opera House interiors and are an appropriate preface to the ribbed shells the visitor will discover as they move up through the building.

Utzon's early drawings showed the concourse supported by a number of columns; Arup suggested that the job could be done by a single span and was keen to investigate a novel form of beam design that would reflect the architect's desire to express honestly the characteristics of the materials used. 'Let the structure speak for itself', Utzon would often say. The design should be bold, simple, on an impressive scale and combine sculptural quality with a clear expression of the forces acting upon it.

Ove Arup proposed a beam that integrated the techniques of folded plate structures and of pre-stressing; in a folded plate, corrugations add strength to the structure. At the ends of a beam, the most effective section

The concourse under construction.

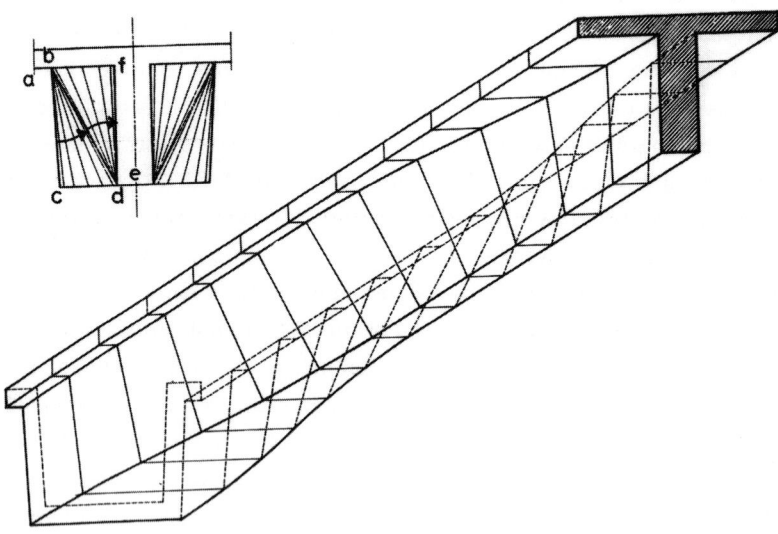

The concourse rib illustrating the change in cross section from 'U' to 'T'.

is a T shape, in the centre of the beam it is a U. Arup's design integrated the two shapes, creating a sculptural and efficient form that Utzon accepted enthusiastically and credited it as 'Ove's invention'. When visiting the site in August 1962, Utzon put his arm around Arup's shoulders and said, 'This is your concourse.'

The design of the beams was carried out by Arup with Povl Ahm, while the complex calculations were all done by Jenkins, assisted by Alan Levy who later went to Sydney to help with supervision on site.

Drawings from the architect were urgently needed on site. However, there were still design problems to be solved which delayed the completion of the detailed drawings. Right from the start the pattern was set – a fast-track building programme requiring a continuous supply of drawings in conflict with the architect's desire to design 'the perfect opera house', frequently changing his mind, and a client, SOHEC, which was undecided in its precise requirements.

SOHEC had been formed in 1957 from members of the old Opera House Committee that had set up the competition. It was a part-time body for a project that needed a full-time client representative.

The committee had great faith in their architect, and Utzon's easy charm would generally win them over. It was made up of 15 members and the chairman, Stan Haviland, the Under Secretary for Local Government, was nicknamed 'Silent' Stan due to his dislike of public pronouncements. Other members included Charles Moses, then the general manager of the Australian Broadcasting Commission (ABC) and Bernhard Heinze, director of the State Conservatorium of Music. SOHEC was advised by three technical advisory panels; one chaired by Professor Ashworth on architectural and constructional aspects, one on traffic chaired by Haviland and one on music and drama chaired by Heinze.

The fact that it was run from the Department of Local Government caused some concern at the Public Works Department. R A Johnson, the Director of the PWD, thought that it should have come under his department as the construction authority for the Government of New South Wales – the Department of Local Government had never before been involved with large-scale building projects. In time, Johnson was to get his way.

SOHEC was an unwieldy structure. In late 1959, Arup wrote to Utzon: 'No one can afford to wait until the Committee formally approves your latest plans for the Major Hall stage area. When your scheme is fully worked out you should send it to Professor Ashworth stressing that he must give immediate authority to go ahead. From past experience, the Committee cannot be summoned in time nor induced to give an opinion positive enough to allow work to proceed in the Major Hall area.'

For Utzon they were the ideal client, despite their propensity to change their minds. They were remarkably patient and allowed him to, in effect, write his own brief. While the committee was criticized for this later by the pro-Utzon campaigners, it suited the architect very well at the time. When he submitted the Red Book to SOHEC in March 1958, its contents were generally accepted and Utzon was asked to progress to working drawings. However, there were continual requests for changes. In June 1958, the administrative area, workshops, rehearsal rooms, dining rooms and orchestra pits were revised. On 4 July, Charles Moses asked for broadcasting facilities to be included; later in the month Utzon submitted drawings which included new designs for the main staircase, cloakrooms and kitchen areas as a result of suggestions from the committee. Even a year later, SOHEC was still requesting major changes. It wanted larger orchestra pits, amendments to the stage lifting machinery and no revolving stage in the Major Hall.

Charles Moses had joined the ABC as a sports reporter and quickly rose through the ranks. His role on the committee perhaps typifies its amateur approach. Despite his job of running the country's broadcasting network, he believed he had been appointed to SOHEC in a personal capacity. He therefore never passed SOHEC papers onto his colleagues at the ABC and, when he retired as general manager in 1965, he remained on the committee rather than handing over to Talbot Duckmanton, his successor. The discovery in 1966 by ABC engineers that the interiors proposed by Utzon were unsuitable for broadcasts was yet another problem that the architect had to face as the pressures built up to his departure.

SOHEC was effectively Utzon's client until the NSW State Government became concerned with progress and decided to take greater control under the Sydney Opera House Act 1960. This named the Minister for Public Works as the constructing authority and empowered him to supervise the work, and enshrined the architect's and engineer's appointments in statute. It also set the cost at A£4,880,000 with each 10 per cent increase requiring the Act to be amended by Parliament, thus ensuring that, in the years to come, the Opera House would became a political football. By naming Utzon as the architect, the Act gave him an enormous amount of protection;

it would have been very difficult for any Minister to fire him.

As the power of SOHEC waned and the Public Works Department (PWD) moved into the driving seat, Utzon's life became less comfortable. He effectively had two clients – SOHEC, which was communicating its rather vague brief, and the Minister for Public Works, who was requesting costings, a schedule of completed drawings and an opening date.

In February 1959, the tender from Civil and Civic Contractors (later to become the construction and development giant Lend Lease) for Stage 1 was accepted by the State Cabinet. At A£1,397,878, it was the lowest bid, some A£200,000 cheaper than Hornibrook Limited, who were later appointed as contractors for Stage 2. The fact that Civil and Civic tendered on incomplete drawings and site surveys was to lead to major disagreements and legal wrangles later.

Meanwhile in Denmark, Utzon had been concentrating on the design of the stage machinery, while Ronald Jenkins and Hugo Mollman in London were carrying out wind tunnel and model tests on the roof shells at Southampton University.

It had been impossible to ascertain the structural feasibility of the competition entry shells using the normal approximations an engineer might use for more traditional structures. It was clear that there were simpler shapes that would solve the engineering problems created by the interplay of the shells. However these would inevitably change the sculptural quality of the competition-winning scheme and it was decided that the engineers should develop a structure that would retain the profile and silhouettes as Utzon had initially conceived them.

The first job was to create a geometric discipline. This they did by using a system of parabolas for the shells, a solution that was as close as they could get to Utzon's free-flowing shapes and allowed Arups to start accurate calculations of the stresses.

In January 1958, the engineers sent drawings to Utzon showing the shells drawn as parabolas. Utzon wrote back to Arup: 'Many thanks for the beautiful "shells"... We are all thrilled with them. They are much better than the competition project.' The engineers also experimented with an ellipsoid geometry, although this resulted in a very similar profile.

The initial structural tests on models at the University of Southampton were on a single reinforced concrete skin. However, as the magnitude of the bending moments became apparent, this was changed to two shells 4ft

(1.2m) apart.

The investigations at Southampton threw up new and unforeseen problems: that the load distributions to the foundations could not be predicted by any analytical techniques then known; that each change to the structure had a knock-on effect, something that is quite normal in structural design but was aggravated by the complexity of the roof and the enormous amount of time needed to investigate each alteration. The Opera House was one of the first large-scale projects to use computers for structural analysis; however, it was a science that was still in its early stages. The only computers available were in university departments or at Ferranti, the leading UK computer company at the time. Calculations that today can be made in fractions of a second then took a couple of weeks. The Arups engineers were learning how to use computers as they went along – without them they would never have been able to carry out credible calculations on the Opera House roofs. Three members of the Stage 2 team went to Southampton for nine months to carry out model tests and to use the University's Pegasus computer.

At this time, there were specific features of Jenkins' solutions that were later changed: the geometry was based either on parabolic or ellipsoidal geometry; the open ends of the shells were closed off with 'louvre' walls and the two halls were each one continuous structure, the shells interlinked at their springing points.

When Utzon was able to look at the design of the roofs in detail, he decided he did not like either the internal appearance or the method of closing up the ends of the shells. This, combined with the fact that the model tests at Southampton were showing some unacceptably high forces near the ground where the shell walls were nearly vertical, was too much for Jenkins. He confessed to Povl Ahm at a party that he could find no mathematical solution to the shells and was no longer interested. As a result of these comments, Ahm started to develop an alternative approach to the roof shapes – if they were viewed as triangular plates meeting at the apex, rather than continuous shells, then analysis would be considerably easier. He took his idea to Ove Arup who, says Ahm, 'was flabbergasted and agreed with me'. Arup accepted this was the way forward and decided to take over the shell design team himself.

Jenkins had become very involved with the fast growing international network of shell specialists, the avant-garde of structural engineering at the time, and was spending a lot of time at conferences and meetings. He was attending one such meeting in The Hague when he received a call from Arup who asked him to come back to the office immediately where he told Jenkins that he was taking over. At a partners meeting in June 1961, Jenkins announced that he had reached a dead end and could see no way forward. He had produced a scheme that would stand up, but Utzon did not like his solution. Jenkins was understandably frustrated; he and Hugo Molman had solved the problem posed by the architect for a structure as he had sketched it after a great deal of skilful and time consuming analysis. He withdrew from the project; Molman was so angry he resigned from Arups completely and returned to work in Denmark. Jenkins and Molman became the first casualties of the Opera House.

Arup had decided that a new team and a new approach was needed. He had previously discussed with Utzon a radical departure from the shell scheme that Jenkins had been investigating, which used a ribbed structure. Following Jenkins' impasse, Arup decided to revive this concept. He therefore asked Jack Zunz, who had set up Arups' South Africa office in 1954 and had recently returned to London, to see what could be done to make the existing double skin scheme viable and, at the same time, to investigate ways in which the structure could be ribbed. These designs were to be studied within the current building shape; as engineers, Arups accepted that it was their job to make the architect's concepts work. 'As far as I was concerned,' says Zunz, 'the geometry was sacrosanct.' John Lethbridge developed the ribbed proposals and Joe Huang worked on the existing scheme.

It was Arups' commitment to meeting the architect's aspirations that tested the engineers' skills to the limit. Had Ashworth and Martin gone to Nervi or Candela, they would probably have told Utzon to change to a more rational structure.

To get Utzon's poetic shapes to stand up, the new engineering team first separated the three sets of shells from each other, forming separate structures for each one. This immediately rationalized the structure compared to the complex interconnected approach taken by Jenkins; it was to have dramatic consequences later when columns, which had already been constructed in Stage 1, had to be partially demolished.

The double skin was essentially a steel structure with concrete internal and external surfaces. Apart from the changes described above, Zunz's design was not radically different from Jenkins' proposal. It was a perfectly

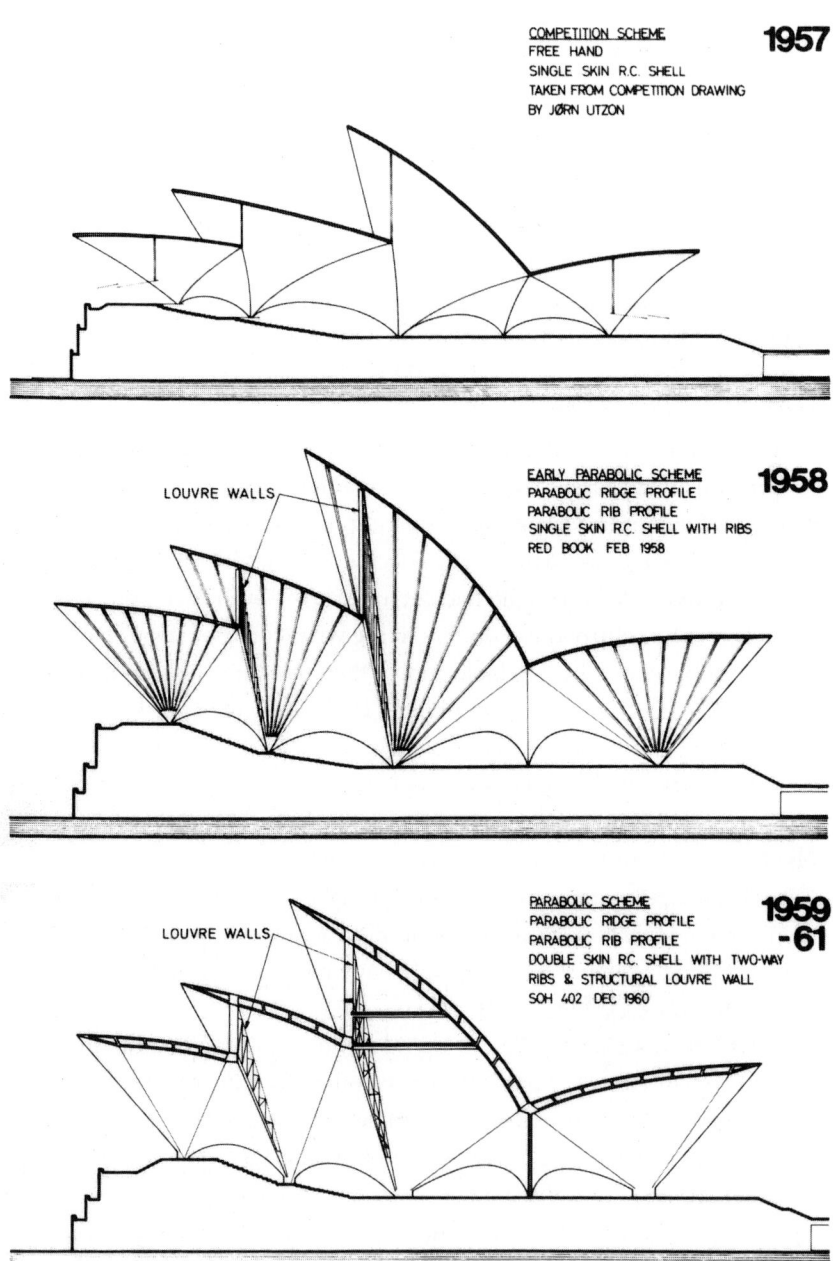

COMPETITION SCHEME
FREE HAND
SINGLE SKIN R.C. SHELL
TAKEN FROM COMPETITION DRAWING
BY JØRN UTZON

1957

LOUVRE WALLS

EARLY PARABOLIC SCHEME
PARABOLIC RIDGE PROFILE
PARABOLIC RIB PROFILE
SINGLE SKIN R.C. SHELL WITH RIBS
RED BOOK FEB 1958

1958

LOUVRE WALLS

PARABOLIC SCHEME
PARABOLIC RIDGE PROFILE
PARABOLIC RIB PROFILE
DOUBLE SKIN R.C. SHELL WITH TWO-WAY
RIBS & STRUCTURAL LOUVRE WALL
SOH 402 DEC 1960

1959 -61

A selection from the dozen different roof solutions produced by Arups.

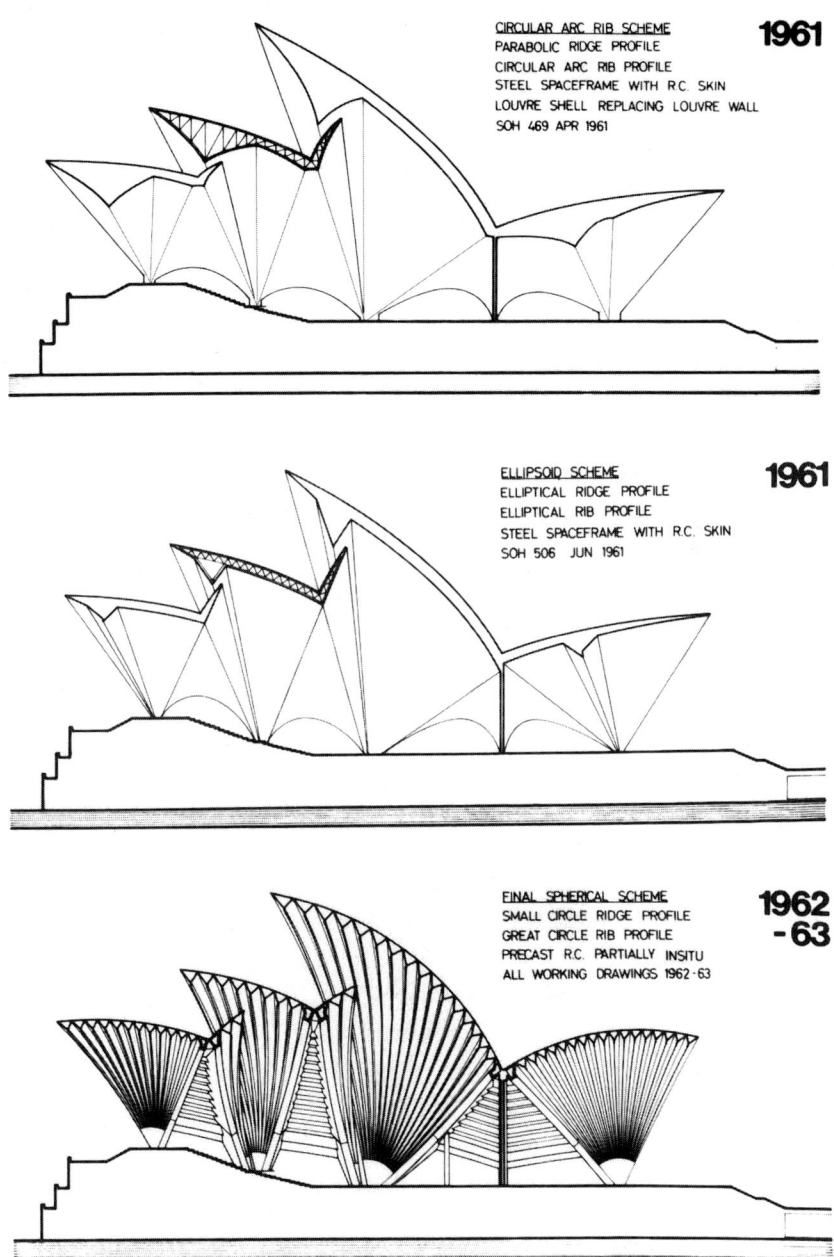

CIRCULAR ARC RIB SCHEME
PARABOLIC RIDGE PROFILE
CIRCULAR ARC RIB PROFILE
STEEL SPACEFRAME WITH R.C. SKIN
LOUVRE SHELL REPLACING LOUVRE WALL
SOH 469 APR 1961

1961

ELLIPSOID SCHEME
ELLIPTICAL RIDGE PROFILE
ELLIPTICAL RIB PROFILE
STEEL SPACEFRAME WITH R.C. SKIN
SOH 506 JUN 1961

1961

FINAL SPHERICAL SCHEME
SMALL CIRCLE RIDGE PROFILE
GREAT CIRCLE RIB PROFILE
PRECAST R.C. PARTIALLY INSITU
ALL WORKING DRAWINGS 1962-63

**1962
-63**

The drawings illustrate how the later solutions were divided into three separate shells.

feasible solution, the changes making it easier to predict the foundation loads. However, the concrete had only a limited structural use and was therefore not being used in what a modernist architect like Utzon would feel to be an 'honest' way.

The ribbed scheme, on the other hand, expressed the properties of concrete dramatically. Zunz had developed Arup's idea of a giant fold in the area of the louvre walls into a scheme made up of a series of smaller ribs that suggested some solution as to how this complicated structure could be built.

In August 1961, Utzon visited the Arup offices and Zunz presented the two proposals. He pointed out that the amended original scheme in steel and concrete would probably be cheaper and quicker than the ribbed scheme. Despite the fact that it would entail considerable alterations to the architecture, that it entailed throwing away three years' work, Utzon plumped for the ribbed structure. 'I don't care what it costs, I don't care what scandal it causes, I don't care how long it takes, but that's what I want,' he said to Arup and to Zunz, who both had great faith in Utzon's judgement on spatial and aesthetic matters.

There followed a series of discussions about the problems of constructing the ribs. Malcolm Nicklin of Macdonald Wagner and Priddle, Arups' engineering representatives in Sydney, was asked to find a site where the roof elements could be wholly or partially assembled on the ground prior to erection. At that time, the concept was to construct a steel framework that would be sprayed with concrete and then stressed together. Because the design was still based on the original geometry, each rib would be different. Zunz, his number two, John Lethbridge, and Utzon discussed this 'geometric straitjacket' in the context of the non-repetitive ribs. Zunz and Lethbridge told Utzon that the only way to create a repetitive structure was with spherical or toroidal geometry. They later discovered this to be incorrect – it could also be done using ellipsoid geometry.

The engineers did not pursue either of these geometries, however, because it would radically alter the entire appearance of the building. Utzon did not have any such qualms.

A month after the discussions with Zunz and Lethbridge, Utzon rang Arup to announce, 'I've solved it!', that he had created the shell geometry from a single sphere. Zunz and Arup went immediately to Hellebæk. Zunz realized that this would indeed solve the problems of repetition of the elements, however it also changed the architecture. It reduced the internal

Model illustrating the relationship of the roof shapes to a sphere.

clearances in areas that were already very congested and it reduced the volumes of the halls. With their faith in Utzon still unshaken, the engineers believed that these were problems their brilliant architect would be able to solve and set about their new task with enthusiasm – the rationalization of the structure was just what they had been asking for.

Utzon had certainly solved many of the difficulties of constructing the shells by his conversion to spherical geometry – but it was a conversion that took place after months of discussion with engineers.

The solution reflected a significant shift in Utzon's idea of the shell finishes. The ribbed structure would provide a very different interior to the smooth concave surface he had discussed with Mikami. However, Utzon had been mightily impressed by the flowing beauty of the concourse beams and this had opened his mind to the concept of the ribs.

In November 1961, Arup wrote a letter to Ashworth explaining that the design of the shells had been resolved. He described how Pier Luigi Nervi's structures are based on repetitive concrete elements. 'We had often discussed the possibility of using such a method with Utzon but the fact that all the shells were different seemed to preclude this. However in the course of our discussions Utzon came up with the idea of making all the shells of a uniform curvature throughout in both directions.'

At around the same time, Utzon wrote enthusiastically to Ashworth: 'We were riding two horses for a long time. The last six months the real solution for everything technically and aesthetically was developed and it was even the cheapest way of making it you could dream of… Of course, all the work during these three years has been the background for arriving at this magnificent solution.'

The local press coverage was robust and frequently critical. The illustrations highlight the change in profile from the competition entry.

Towards the end of 1961 Arup, then aged 67, became ill. He suffered from low blood pressure and this, exacerbated by stress, made him prone to fainting attacks. The difficulties of designing the roofs and the pressure of the tight schedule, compounded by the fact that the firm was financially on the line, took their toll. He went to Bad Gadstein in Austria to recuperate and was forced to cancel a trip to Sydney that had been planned for March. Zunz and Utzon went and presented the Yellow Book, the updated version of the Red Book illustrating the new shell designs. The change in shape caused a certain amount of comment in the press. Utzon tried to play down the significance of the changes. 'The silhouette hasn't altered,' he told the *Sydney Morning Herald*, 'detailed drawings people are seeing now make the roof shell look steeper than on models and on the finished building.' However, whatever the public relations angle might have been, it is clear that the profile of the building had changed radically; the smoothly-curving shells of the competition entry had been exchanged for the upright arches of the spherical solution.

In the same article, Utzon is quoted as saying: 'There has been some misunderstanding along lines that the engineer had to take over and make something that could stand up. This is not so. We are working beautifully together. You won't be able to separate structure from architecture when it has been finished.'

This cordial relationship shines through in an undated letter that was sent some time in early 1962 while Arup was recuperating and just before the visit to Sydney. Utzon wrote to him:

'We think of you and Lis [Arup's wife] daily and talk about you – a standing remark in the office is we wonder what Ove would have done with this problem.

'I have missed you greatly here recently in the development of the details, but I think everything has gone the way you would have wanted and the side shells follow exactly the way you sketched them in the letter to me. Everything is now very beautiful and belong to the same family as regards form, conception and quality – all is now nothing but good news. We have been extremely busy – I cannot recall a similar burst of energy in the office.'

Bill Laurie, an architect and a member of the Technical Advisory Panel, had been at Hellebæk and there had been a dress rehearsal for the meetings in Sydney. 'Mr Laurie was very pleased as he left yesterday and mentioned that he was deeply impressed by yours and my joint work.'

The architect may have been satisfied with the structure, but the Government decided, 'because of the novel design of the work, the method of construction, and the very great cost involved, that it should not rely on the advice of one firm of consultants', but that alternative advice should be sought to reassure them of the stability of the proposed structure. In August 1962, the Government asked Arups to recommend another consultant who could comment sensibly on their structures. Zunz suggested Yves Guyon, a French civil engineer who was a pioneer in prestressed concrete design and one of the most distinguished engineers of his generation. Guyon gave the structure the thumbs up. 'The structural scheme is basically sound and attainable provided the members are of the correct dimensions and reinforced adequately... The erection procedure which has been devised is in my opinion sound.'

Arups were not the only ones to undergo such scrutiny. Utzon had been very impressed by the interior of the Philharmonie in Berlin designed by Hans Scharoun, which was then under construction, where the audience surrounded the orchestra. At the same time, he was not keen on Jordan's 'shoe box' approach and wanted something more in keeping with the rest of the architecture of the Opera House. So he consulted Professor Lothar Cremer, Director of the Institut fur Technische Akustik in Berlin, and Werner Gabler, an architect specializing in acoustics, who had worked together on the Philharmonie and asked them to provide a second opinion to Jordan on the acoustics of the Minor and Major Halls. Jordan was deeply unhappy with this arrangement – but he did not resign.

CHAPTER 3
THE MOVE TO SYDNEY

The white tiled surfaces of the sail-like shells are one of the great architectural triumphs of the Opera House. The glistening forms respond lyrically to the changing Sydney sun; the intricate arrangement of matt and gloss tiles helps to define the curves of the roof and create a living surface, the whiteness of which contrasts with the darker colours of the surrounding city.

Utzon had been inspired by the domes of Islamic mosques, and tiles he had seen in China and Japan, which he described in the Red Book as 'the homelands of the art of ceramics'. Equally, he was influenced by the durability and weather resistance of glazed tiles in the extreme Australian climate. Utzon was unable to find a standard product that met his requirements so he set out to produce a special tile that met his very personal brief: a tile that, when applied over the huge areas of the Opera House shells, would 'produce colour, surface texture and pattern required by me'.

Utzon had worked before with the Swedish firm of Hoganas, located some 20km from Halsingborg, and they were the natural choice to develop the tile. They experimented with a range of materials, finishes and shapes, and built a full-scale mock up of a corner of a shell which showed that the most appropriate layout on the double-curved structure was a square tile laid diagonally. Tests revealed that the normal pressed tile gave a very dull effect, while extruded tiles gave a livelier reflection. Despite the fact that Hoganas spent nearly two years developing the tiles, SOHEC insisted, for political reasons, that the contract should go out to tender. Utzon was relieved when Hoganas's price came in cheaper than the two local companies who were also invited to submit.

Utzon alighted on a tile with a white transparent glaze and an uneven texture for the main areas. The texture provided a diffused and softer reflection of the sun than the hard image created by a standard glaze finish.

The diagonally laid, 5in (120mm) square tiles were designed in narrow chevrons that responded to the geometry of the ribs. The edge of the Vs were delineated by matt, off-white tiles.

Initially, Utzon had intended to fix tiles directly to the shell structure. Now that the structure had changed, this solution was no longer feasible. The architect then proposed that they should be cast into the ribs before erection, but the engineers felt that this would cause insurmountable difficulties in waterproofing the structure, gaining access to the ribs to fix them together, insulating the roof and ensuring a smooth continuous surface.

Zunz suggested separating the two elements and created the concept of the 'tile lids'. These would be prefabricated, precast concrete units onto which the tiles would be bonded in factory conditions.

The idea of the lids was confirmed in a technical report produced for Hoganas by Professor Ove Petersson of The Royal Institute of Technology, Stockholm. Prefabricated tile panels were in general use in Sweden where the hard winters made outside fixing impossible for several months of the year. Generally, tiles would be laid face down in a tray and a cementatious mixture poured onto the backs.

This was essentially the process followed at the Opera House, but as with many of the elements of the building, the solution was not quite so simple. The panels were curved for a start. The structure of each lid comprised a backing of ferro-cement, a method of creating strong light panels developed by Pier Luigi Nervi which involved a cement and sand mix reinforced with three layers of galvanized steel mesh. The tile and slab were just 1¼in (30mm) thick; a cruciform stiffening rib increased the depth of the whole unit to 6in (150mm).

Utzon wanted a recess between each tile in order to define the edges; this would normally be created by pouring sand between the laid tiles and spraying with water before pouring the concrete backing. However, the contractors were finding that the sand was adhering to the concrete. They were at a loss for a solution until a carpenter on site offered to help them out for 'fifty quid'. He suggested they run heated animal glue along the joints – when the panels were heat-cured, the glue would melt and leave a clean recessed space. The suggestion worked and production of the 4,253 lids commenced.

Around a million tiles were used. The mind-numbing job of drawing the layout of each individual tile had fallen to the Arups engineers. This is a job that would have normally been carried out by the architect, however it was clearly impossible for Utzon's office to do the complex geometric work within the timescale. There were 41 types of edge tile and the type number of each edge tile was indicated on the drawings. In correspondence, Jack Zunz, whose letters often displayed a wry humour, particularly when situations were tense, suggested the work was affecting the sanity of his staff: '...the drudgery in drawing Utzon's tile lids or the 150 different special end segments for the shell ribs is very severe. In fact, I am advised that after one man has done four of these end segments he is suicide material.'

The design of the tiles was discussed in detail on Boxing Day 1962 at a crucial meeting that took place as Utzon set off for Australia to open his office there. The meeting marked a turning point in the project and in the relationship between the architect and his engineers.

Arups were planning to open a Sydney office to coincide with Utzon's arrival. This was to be headed by Michael Lewis, a no-nonsense South African who had worked in London with Ove Arup and Partners during the 1950s, and set up the Arups South Africa office with Zunz. Arup and Zunz knew they could trust Lewis; he was a senior member of staff and technically sound. However, Lewis would only agree to take on the job if his brief also included setting up a permanent Arups office in Sydney.

When the firm took on the Opera House job there was no plan to open an office in Sydney at all. The local engineers Macdonald Wagner and Priddle were hired to act as Arups' representatives. They were highly experienced in the management of large civil engineering projects and the relationship between the two firms was cordial and worked very effectively. When Zunz took over the project, he thought it was essential to have an Arups presence in Sydney: he wanted someone to lead the team as well as engineers who had worked on the designs in London, and who knew something about the project. The partners of Ove Arup and Partners were not keen on another overseas branch – the existing ones were seen as financial strain enough. The firm then was a traditional partnership and each of them shared financial responsibility; the finances were fairly stretched because of the Opera House, which, it was thought at the time, would produce a loss. Arup himself was not at all keen, but Lewis won the day.

Announcing the move, Zunz informed Stan Haviland that the team of at least four engineers would be 'among our leading lights'. The group included the young Peter Rice, who was to become one of the most celebrated

The podium, Stage 1, under construction in July 1963. The seating banks of the two auditoria are clearly visible.

engineers of his generation and was already making a reputation within Arups for his brilliant structural analyses. Lewis was to run the office and would concentrate on the design side with direct contact with the architects; Rice would play a crucial role in the erection of the shells.

The Boxing Day meeting took place in the Aerial Hotel close to Heathrow airport and was attended by Utzon, Arup, Zunz, Mikami and Lewis. The end of 1962 was a critical period for the project. The Stage 2 contract had been let to M R Hornibrook Property Limited in October. On Arup's recommendation, the Government had agreed, somewhat unwillingly, to nominate them instead of going out to tender. Arup convinced the Public Works Department (PWD) that on a project of such complexity, it was essential that design and construction were totally integrated. The engineers were under pressure to provide drawings so that work could start on site and, at the same time, were embroiled in legal arguments with Civil and Civic who were claiming additional costs on Stage 1. A conglomeration of factors – the premature start on site, a too low tender by Civil and Civic and continual changes to the design – meant that the contractor was losing money. After months of argument they succeeded in claiming a further A£1,232,000 on top of the A£1,397,929 they had tendered in January 1959. This was a huge amount when one considers that the Government understood that the cost of the completed building would be just A£12.5million.

Utzon planned to take a break en route to Australia; he had closed up his office at Hellebæk and was not scheduled to arrive in Sydney until March the next year. There was so much to be done and no one to contact from the architect's office. Zunz begged him to delay his trip, but Utzon was adamant and the Boxing Day meeting at Heathrow, between connecting flights, was set up to clear as many outstanding issues as possible. It started at 3.20pm and continued, with dinner in between, until 11.00pm. Zunz had a list of some 63 items that required decisions from Utzon, including queries about the tiles and tile panel design, such as the ridge detail, the depth of the joints and the details of the bottom edge of the tile lids.

The weather was particularly cold and the hotel's heating inadequate to its task; Arup was quite ill and spent some of the meeting with his feet in a hot bath. But the spirit of the meeting was cheerful. Mikami relates, 'The atmosphere of this extraordinary meeting was extremely amicable, and Jørn was making jokes all the time during the discussions.' Utzon sketched a symbol on a piece of paper, a circle within a square, two diagonal lines and one central vertical one. Out of this shape he could trace U for Utzon, Z for Zunz and Y for Yuzo Mikami, saying it was a sign of perfect collaboration.

While Utzon and his family travelled across America and holidayed in Tahiti, he was almost completely out of touch with the project. Apart from a letter from the Windjammer Inn in Miami with the postscript, 'You can reach me here until 11/1,' and a letter written by Lis Utzon from Grand Bahama Island dated 11 January, Arups heard nothing of Utzon until he arrived in Sydney. In the note from Miami, Utzon sketched changes to the tile edge detail and an alteration to the side shells.

Arups were urgently preparing drawings for Stage 2 for Corbet Gore, Hornibrook's director of construction at the Opera House, so that work could start on site. For the previous year, Gore had been working closely with Arups developing methods of construction and had spent three months in London familiarizing himself with their thinking. It was a fruitful relationship. At the time Zunz wrote, 'I have personally worked closely with Corbet over the past two or three months. Quite apart from his technical acumen and enthusiasm, we are all most taken with his attitude to the job and with his sincerity of purpose. While very often one talks about the desirability or otherwise of having a contractor in the design team, we feel that in this instance they are really with us.' Gore is viewed by many of those involved with the Opera House as an heroic figure. Large of frame and personality, he drove the construction programme with grit, flair and imagination.

Utzon made his way to Australia travelling westwards; Lewis flew in the opposite direction, stopping over in Israel. While sightseeing, he was hit by a bus and his leg was badly broken. He was in hospital for five weeks, delaying his arrival in Sydney until 5 April, a month after Utzon got there.

Just four members of staff from the Hellebæk office moved to Australia: Jon Lundberg, Mogens Prip-Buus, Jacob Kielland-Brandt and Oktai Nayman. They arrived at the end of January and set up an office on site at Bennelong Point adjacent to the Arups site hut with a connecting door between the two.

Zunz and Arup were in Sydney at the beginning of March for the tedious proceedings of the Civil and Civic arbitration. On 4 March, while flying from Tahiti to Sydney, Utzon received an invitation via the airplane's radio to lunch on the Royal Yacht Britannia and meet the Queen who was on a state visit to Australia. Landing at Sydney, Utzon was whisked to the regal reception without having time to change from his travelling clothes.

Zunz was not amused. He described Utzon's arrival in the Opera House oral history tapes: '…and lo and behold God appears from Heaven.' He described how Utzon arrived from Tahiti in the morning and then, '…in the afternoon he comes onto the site and starts complaining about some things he wasn't informed about. I mean, there was no one we could contact!'

Zunz's humour had not been improved by the Civil and Civic case. He and Arup felt that they were taking the blame for political decisions over which they had no control. Many of the problems faced by Civil and Civic could be traced back to the early start insisted upon by Joe Cahill. Ove Arup had advised against this, but accepted that unless a start was made the job would probably never go ahead. Arups felt that the resulting problems were reflecting badly on the competence of the practice. They were becoming fed up with being blamed for increases in costs when they were pressed by the politicians to provide estimates based on inadequate information. Preliminary guesses were turned into firm undertakings and, when they were exceeded, 'accusing eyes were cast in our direction.'

They wanted to change the arrangement where they were responsible for all the consultants except the quantity surveyors, although they were unable to direct them without reference to the architect.

In a hard-hitting statement to the Government dated 26 March 1963, Arups wrote: 'The time has come to cast away pretence and make-belief and face the facts about the organisation of the job, of who is responsible for what, and accept the consequences in the allocation of executive power and fees.'

They described the arrangement whereby all the specialist consultants were responsible to the structural consultants, however, Arups complained that it was frequently a gamble whether they were able to obtain sufficient fees from the client to pay the consultants. On top of that they were not being paid any additional fees for the trouble, responsibility or financial risk. 'This situation is absurd and cannot be allowed to continue.' The engineers had all the responsibilities, but no power.

Arups had, they said, done far more for the job than could possibly be construed as falling under their responsibilities as structural engineers. Because of the complexity of the geometry, electronic computers were used: '...to enable us to translate this geometry into working details. Consequently it has unavoidably fallen to us to work out many of the essentially architectural details, such as, for instance, the tile lids, the dimensions of which in a normal job would have been supplied by the architect, and for which we have to make about 350 drawings. This does not reflect on the architect, and in no way diminishes his difficulties. It is just that owing to the difficult geometry and the scale of the job which necessitates considerations of secondary stresses and temperature movements which can normally be neglected, this is not a job where the architect in the usual way can supply us with outlines, for which we then do the calculations and detail drawings.'

The engineers were concerned at their own soaring costs. To the end of December 1962, they had expended 175,000 man-hours on the job and reckoned they would need a further 300,000 hours to get to the end of Stage 2. They had 55 engineers and their aides working on the project; the effort involved was having a detrimental effect on all the firm's activities.

'In spite of all this we want to make it quite clear we do not aspire to become co-principal with Utzon nor do we recommend such a course.' Arup was fulsome in his praise of the architect: 'He is a brilliant designer – one of the best, and probably the best of any I have come across in my long experience of working with architects – and he has a remarkable ability quickly to understand the essence of other technical disciplines as they impinge on his architectural conception.'

Despite these complimentary comments, Utzon took huge offence at the rest of the statement, particularly with regard to the tile lids. He was upset that it appeared that Arups were now doing the architecture as well as the engineering.

He seemed to resent the fact that Mikami, who had worked for him in Hellebæk, had joined Arups. Mikami had been responsible for some of the tile lid drawings. When Zunz sent some of the Japanese architect's drawings from London to Lewis in Sydney, he suggested they should not be shown to Utzon; if he recognized them as Mikami's drawings they would be likely to 'cloud the issue'.

As soon as Utzon arrived in Sydney, the engineers gave him a summary of the architectural decisions taken by them between January and March 1963 while he was out of contact. But on 26 March, John Nutt – a young Australian at Arups' office in London but who would later move to Sydney – wrote to Robert Kelman in the Sydney office:

'Bob, Utzon here appears to be out of touch with what we have been doing over the last couple of months. Would you bring him up to date? A lot of information has been scheduled and a lot of reinforcing details drawn and listed and we don't want to change this. All we have done up till now has been on the lines laid out by Utzon before he went out of circulation.... We have enough on our plate keeping up with major points rather than changing minor points that have in general already been agreed.'

With hindsight this may be seen as the early signs of the deteriorating relationship between the architect and the engineers. However, for the time being, Utzon and Lewis were keen to patch things up. On 10 May, Lewis wrote a memo to London: 'Jørn without any prompting from me made a declaration of his high regard for you and Jack and for all the members of Ove Arup and Partners and he has expressed his concern for the possibility of any rift in the relationship between the two firms.'

On 13 May, Ove Arup sent a memo to Lewis which, three years later, Utzon claimed was proof that Arups were conspiring to take the job over from him.

In the memo Arup describes four ways in which the next stages of the contract could be administered:

'1. We can insist on completing Stage 2 in its pure undiluted form and when Hornibrook are off the site we can hand over to Utzon. The Government will undoubtedly be strongly opposed to this because the job may not be finished in 1970 – it mightn't be in any case but at least we should try!

2. We can allow ourselves to drift into a situation where we are de facto administering the whole completion of the project without having any powers to direct the work which would be mechanical, electrical and "architectural" and without being paid for it to boot. This in essence is the pattern which had evolved since the beginning of the job. This should be strongly avoided – we must learn from past mistakes and must not let ourselves drift into what could become an impossibly chaotic situation.

3. We can hand Stage 2 over to Utzon now – we would carry on directing work on the superstructure for the time being on his behalf. This would allow him to set up an organisation on the site for the future having regard to the complex operations which have to be carried out before its completion.

4. We can administer Stage 2 and offer to continue with the whole contract till it is complete. In that case, we would, however, have to set up a special team to deal with this and we would have to be paid for it, and the situation where we are joint principal consultants should be given due recognition.

'Of these four possibilities Number 1 will not be tolerated by the clients, Number 2 cannot in any circumstances be tolerated by us, so that it is a choice between 3 and 4. This choice is mainly a choice for Utzon, because he is at the moment the principal consultant and we are only too happy if he will in fact exercise his rights and undertake the duties belonging to that position. The question is, however, whether he will in fact be willing and able to set up the necessary organisation on the site to run Stages 2 and 3.'

Arup suggested that the choice was between 3 and 4, 'unless Utzon or the clients can put forward an alternative which is equally clear-cut'.

'This matter should be discussed immediately with Utzon because when the Minister comes here on 27th May, it is sure to come up, and we must know Utzon's views beforehand.'

However, Lewis had written to Arup and Zunz, with a copy to Utzon, telling them not to raise the topic of altering the contract with Norman Ryan, Labor Minister for Public Works. He wrote that he was in full agreement with the London office analysis of the situation and that 3 and 4 were the only practical options. 'We would be over-reaching ourselves even contemplating Number 4 and I am strongly inclined towards Number 3. This is what Utzon wants in any case. Jørn is fully aware of the problems which confront him and has hired extra staff: two Australian architects in the drawing office and one administrative assistant who is an architect.'

However, Arups in London were clearly concerned about Utzon's management. Ove Arup's memo had been drafted by Zunz; the draft, but not the final text, suggested that Number 4 would be the best option for the job, 'having regard to Utzon's administrative shortcomings'. In a letter to Zunz a year later, Lewis wrote 'He [Utzon] felt that Ove had directly and indirectly been responsible for a feeling which exists that he is incapable of administering a contract of this scale and complexity.'

At the end of May 1963, Arup and Zunz were dismayed to receive a letter from Utzon written in an uncharacteristically formal and frosty tone. Gone was the friendly 'Dear Ove' or 'Dear Jack'; instead he wrote to 'Dear Sirs'. Utzon's letter set out his thoughts on 'the future procedure concerning the administration and Ove Arup and Partners' participation in the Sydney Opera House construction'. He said that he would be dealing with the structural problems on Stage 3, the interiors and the windows, and he would be providing the necessary contract documents, recommend the contract procedure, negotiate all contracts and superintend all works.

The items that applied to Arups were just the cladding and paving on Stage 1, the structure of the Major and Minor Halls, the glass walls, the structures of the experimental theatre and rehearsal room ceilings, waterproofing and some additional minor structures.

Tensions were also building up between Arups' London office and their team in Sydney as a result of decisions that had been made while Utzon was on his travels. A frustrated Zunz wrote to Lewis that there were suggestions 'emanating from Utzon and/or Gore, possibly aided and abetted by you' to make major amendments to the superstructure which had already been designed and drawn up.

'This job has strained our technical, financial and human resources almost to breaking point. It is probably not unfair to say that Utzon's office has been inoperative for six months having regard to the dead periods before he packed up, the journey to Sydney, and the time it has taken to re-establish as a working unit. He made the decision to move unilaterally and in the face of my pleadings to delay his departure so that all ends could be tied up. He may not have realized the seriousness of vesting certain powers in us during this dead period.'

Morale in Fitzroy Street was low. Zunz was concerned that the only way to maintain the enthusiasm of staff was to be able to see some orderly way of completing the project, and that changes at this stage would set up a chain reaction involving new theories, programmes, schedules, drawings and designs that 'would prevent this building ever being completed'.

Relations with Lewis were tense; Prip-Buus believed Arups were undermining Utzon's office with frequent requests for information which they were unable to provide. The door between the two offices was bricked up and Utzon gave instructions that the engineers would require prior appointments to meet with the architects.

In his diaries published in 2000, Prip-Buus makes continual disparaging remarks about Arups and the British. Anglo-Danish relations were not improved when the Queen visited the site and failed to speak to Prip-Buus: 'She and Philip came on a visit, unannounced but accompanied by a security agent, and she was discourteous enough only to nod to us.'

Zunz tried to patch things up with Utzon. On 23 August 1962, he wrote 'There have been undertones and undercurrents in some correspondence which has not been the case before. We find ourselves out of step not only with you but also with Mick [Lewis] and Bob [Kelman]. Help us to restore the feeling of understanding, co-operation and friendship which I know really exists between our offices.'

Utzon responded in initially placatory terms – he returned temporarily to 'Dear Jack': 'I was very pleased when I got your kind letter because as you say in it, there has not been the same spirit between us as we have had before,' – but he went on to explain a view of the problems that must have done little to allay Lewis's fears:

'Only I, I am sure, can possibly visualize the final picture of the Opera House. All consultants, all contractors, every craftsman should in a way, understand this in order to enable us, together, to achieve the perfect building.

'I think my mistake has been that every time when you have had new people coming into the scheme, as now for instance Mr Lewis and Mr Perry etc I have not been able, even if I have tried hard, to make them understand what a great danger there lies in side-tracking and not even the smallest detail, which, in the newcomers' minds has no importance, could from the architect's point of view, be left over or taken carelessly, because a number of details always add up to a total picture.'

He went on to describe how the success of the two firms' collaboration to date had forced the best out of each of them, and in a 'higher way' than any

Michael Lewis with Ove Arup and Jack Zunz.

other collaboration he could think of between architect and engineer. However, he had not found quite the same sort of mutual respect with Lewis. 'Ultimati fait accomplets [sic]', and 'this is not the architect's business – are bad things and that does not do well in a fine collaboration.'

Arups Sydney office was overwhelmed with getting the shells up and was simultaneously trying to get information on the interiors from Utzon. In September 1963, Lewis wrote to Arup and Zunz: 'We have received no details from Utzon, although he has told me on numerous occasions over the past three months that I can expect drawings in 2 weeks' time.' Lewis said that he was unwilling to start work on detailed drawings until the design was resolved, and was concerned that he had a staff of six eager to get on with the job but nothing to do.

However, the problems with the relationship with Lewis were fundamental. He had not been party to the wonderful working relationship between engineers and architects at Hellebæk and was not in awe of Utzon. Lewis wrote to Zunz at the time, 'Unlike you and Ove I have not learnt to love Jørn yet and I doubt very much that I ever will.'

Corbet Gore described Utzon as being like Sir Christopher Wren, wanting to change things as though the concrete structure was medieval masonry. In Denmark, with its strong craft tradition and smaller scale projects, this was how he could work. In one of the most complex building projects the world had ever seen, there would inevitably be those who were frustrated by Utzon's frequent changes of mind. Stage 1 and Stage 2 were driven by the structure and managed by Arups. Stage 3 would be driven by the architectural design. Utzon's office was small, very bright but inexperienced. The question was, could they deliver?

The tough pragmatism of Sydney, where the public and politicians wanted to see results and where progress was monitored in the full glare of publicity, was in stark contrast to the silent beech forests of Hellebæk. The secluded studio where Arup and Utzon would earnestly debate architectural and philosophical issues was fading into a romantic past.

'That romantic view is, however, a very real view,' says Lewis, 'and that's what I walked in on. I said – please, in what way are they gods? Why is everyone seduced around here? And I suppose that also affected my approach.'

What Lewis walked into was a project where, a full five years after the architect's appointment, no information existed from which anything other than the structure could be built.

CHAPTER 4
A QUART INTO A PINT POT

The erection of the shells was programmed to take two years during which time Utzon needed to prepare designs for the interiors, in particular for the Major and Minor Halls, as well as for the huge glass walls that would close off the ends of the shells. In fact, due to the complex design and construction of the shells, erection took over three years, so Utzon had a year's grace in which to complete his programme.

Lewis's role was to concentrate on the engineering design of Stage 3, while his on-site team of Ian McKenzie assisted by Peter Rice, Bob Kelman and John Nutt supervised the construction work on Stage 2. Arups moved into a site office at the bottom of the Tarpeian Steps in front of the Botanic Gardens, which had been vacated by Civil and Civic. Hornibrook set up their site office within the podium.

Before Hornibrook could start building the roof structure, some adjustments were required to the columns supporting the shells. These drove down through the podium to the foundations beneath. When the podium had been built, the columns were designed on the basis of the information available at the time, but when Zunz divided the roof into three separate structures and introduced the ribbed scheme, higher design loads were imposed. This meant that columns and floors that had already been constructed required strengthening and additional piers needed to be placed under existing columns.

It was a major task. Kelman wrote to Zunz in London: 'The magnitude of this work in rebuilding these columns is fantastic and could slow the whole progress of Stage 2 down, unless dealt with pretty drastically now.' It had taken two men with jack picks nearly two weeks to cut away just one yard of the high strength concrete. To speed things up, Hornibrook suggested using explosives and called in a specialist subcontractor to blow the tops off the columns.

The explosions were very loud and to mask the noise it was decided to detonate them at 8.30 in the morning at the height of rush hour when the din of the traffic might put the suspicious Sydney press off the scent. The ruse worked for some time until a lump of concrete landed on a passing ferry. The next day the headlines proclaimed another 'Opera House bungle'.

The demolition process, described by Kelman as being like peeling a banana because of the way the reinforcement folded back on itself after the explosion, took almost four months. Some twenty columns required strengthening, their girth increased in some cases to a massive 8ft (2.4m) square. Although to the outside world the site seemed to be a disaster zone, those on site were more optimistic – at least they knew where they were going and how they were going to build the troublesome shells.

Hornibrook set up a factory for the precast units on the site and developed the construction methods. The roof structure required 2,400 precast rib units and more than 4,000 tile panels. These were cast in steel-framed formwork with a plywood lining. Hornibrook experimented with resin coatings – a product that was not commercially available at the time – to give a smooth finish. The quality of concrete finish consumed Utzon at this stage in the contract. He had generally been unhappy with the finishes on Stage 1 and was keen to ensure Hornibrook understood his requirements. The problem of the quality of concrete was compounded by cultural differences: in Europe an 'exposed concrete finish' was seen as a high quality architectural surface, in Australia it virtually meant 'unfinished'. Utzon's obsession was such that Peter Myers, one of the Australian architects in Utzon's office, recalls him weeping when shuttering was removed from a perfect pour, the concrete surface free of any bubbles or blemishes.

The huge pedestals – the heavily reinforced bases where the ribs converge – were cast in situ and then the 15ft (4.5m) precast rib sections were lifted into place by one of the three tower cranes that travelled on rail bridges, progressing along the axis of the shell as each section was completed. The rib sections were supported during construction by the previously completed arch on one side and a special steel arch developed by Corbet Gore on the other. The 'erection arch', as it became known, had telescopic sections that could be adjusted to suit the differing rib sizes, and ball joints at the top and bottom so that its angle could be changed as it moved along the building.

As each rib section was lowered into place it was given a coat of epoxy to bond it to the section below. The use of epoxy in concrete construction was in its infancy, but it had the advantage not just of strength, but of quick setting time. Utzon did not want the joints between the rib sections to be too visible, and a traditional concrete joint would have slowed down construction since it would need 24 hours to cure before stressing. One section a day was too slow. After numerous tests both in England at the Cement and Concrete Association and the University of New South Wales, suitable methods of preparation and application were developed and Hornibrook felt confident that it could be safely used on the Opera House.

The sections were then stressed temporarily using an ingenious technique developed by the contractor. Nine ducts were cast into the sections, three at each corner of the rib, through which cables were threaded, each with a 'flying wedge' that could be pushed up through the duct but could not be pulled down. The cables were stressed three at a time, each set leapfrogging the other so that the first two sections were stressed with three cables, with jacks at the bottom and flying wedges at the top, and the next group of three stressing the third section; the first three could then be released and moved on up the arch. Once all the sections were in place the permanent stressing

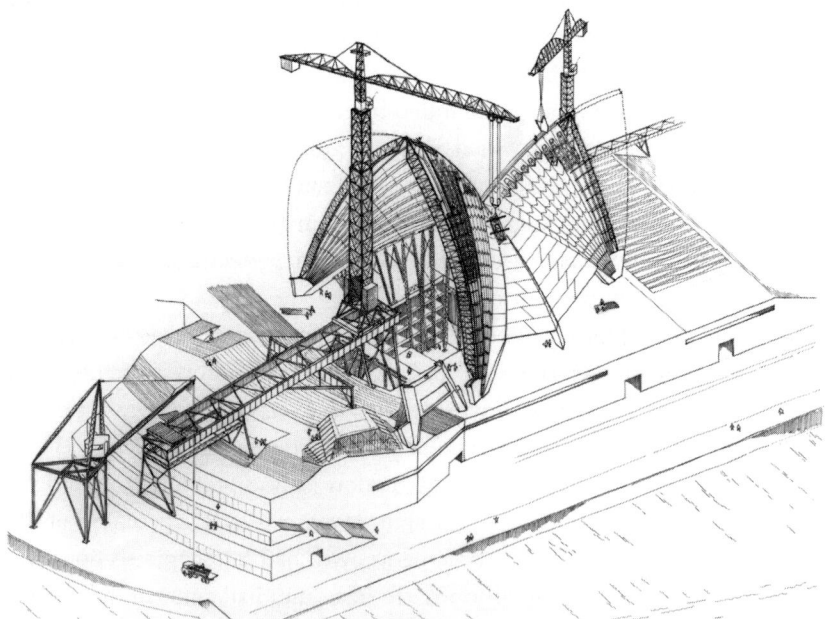

The shells under construction drawn by Yuzo Mikami in 1963 – the erection arch can be seen supporting the partially completed roof; the crane moves along the central rail.

One of the rib sections is lifted into place; the erection arch is visible in the background.

was carried out.

If the complete roof was to be constructed successfully in this cumulative way it was essential to work out the precise location in space of each element as it went up, so that any necessary corrective measures could be taken in good time. However, when the first side shell was erected it took the engineers a full four weeks to determine its exact location. They realized a quicker method of calculation was required if the Opera House was to be finished in their lifetime. Peter Rice, John Nutt and surveyor, Michael Elphick, therefore developed a special computer program so that they could check each day's work overnight. Metal pins were inserted in the concrete units in known locations; once erected the positions of the pins were checked by theodolite. These survey readings would be dispatched by taxi to Australian General Electric's computer in York Street, Sydney, fed into the program and run overnight. The precise erected positions of the ribs would be delivered to site the next morning. The engineers were then able to compare the actual and the theoretical positions of the pins and make on-site adjustments to compensate for the 'give' of the scaffolding or erection arch.

The completed ribs fan out from the pedestal base.

This was a unique and groundbreaking use of computer technology.

The program took some time to develop but luckily did not hold up construction – the engineers were given a breather by a three-month crane-drivers' strike, one of the many that afflicted the site, and by the time Bennelong Point was back at work the program was up and running.

Once the ribs were prestressed, the ridge beam was dropped into place; this was secured to the ribs in order to create a pointed arch spanning between the pedestals. As each rib was positioned it was bolted to the previous one; once they were all erected the sections were prestressed laterally to create a continuous structure. The joints were made watertight using lead flashing across the joints between the ribs.

Next the tile lids were lifted into position. This process required the same accurate surveying as the ribs. The lids had deformed slightly during curing when they had been hung vertically in the drying yard, so detailed adjustment had to be made during construction to ensure a spherical finish. Some 6,000 phosphor bronze bolts were cast into the ribs. The surveyors, with theodolites, determined the precise position in space of the top of each bolt and then, using the same computer techniques employed on the erection of the ribs, calculated where the panel would sit in relation to the bolt and how many washers would be needed to pack it up to the required level.

The erection of the tile lids was not finally completed until March 1967, a year after Utzon resigned from the project.

While the main structure of the Opera House was being built as the architect and engineers had envisaged it, the design development of what would be built beneath the soaring vaults was running into major problems.

There were several strands to the saga that would end in the final confrontation with Davis Hughes, Minister for Public Works in the new Liberal/Country Party Coalition State Government. On the architectural side, the problems were the layout of the Major Hall, the design of the auditoria ceilings and the design of the glass walls. The last two were frustrating design problems that damaged the relationship between Arup and Utzon, but which could, with time, be solved. The first was more intractable, the problem created by Utzon's very first decision to place the auditoria side by side and his later decision to change to spherical geometry. The constraints imposed by the reduced volume above the podium meant he did not have enough space to fit in the required number of seats in an arrangement that was, in the end, acceptable to his client.

The tile lids are hung out to dry.

A tile lid is hoisted into position.

Utzon's changing relationship with the engineers must be seen in the context of the Government's desire to exert greater control on the process of building the Opera House and to change the roles of the various client bodies. In September 1962, the Labor Premier who succeeded Cahill, Robert J Heffron, told SOHEC that, in future, the committee was to act only as an advisory committee to the Minister for Public Works rather than as the client for the project. This altered the position that had existed since 1960 when, despite the Sydney Opera House Act making the Minister the constructing authority, the Premier had been content to allow SOHEC to continue to function as an executive body with substantial powers to make decisions. The reason for this shift in administrative hierarchy was that the Labor Government was becoming concerned about rising costs and wanted to find out what was going on.

The Director of Public Works wrote to Stan Haviland, chairman of SOHEC, in October 1962: 'The procedures have not proved to be entirely satisfactory, particularly from the point of view of the Minister being kept fully informed by the Committee.' The Minister, Norman Ryan, was particularly concerned at the substantial increase in the latest estimates, which suggested that the completed building would cost A£12.5million, and that the need to go before Parliament each time there was a hike in the costs gave ammunition to the Liberal opposition and was politically damaging to the Government.

In June 1963, Ryan visited London and met Arup and Zunz. Zunz wrote to Lewis: 'He [Ryan] is quite adamant about his assumption of power... there is no doubt that all major decisions will flow from his department.'

It was at this meeting that the changes in Arup's agreement were discussed, a conversation that was later misinterpreted by Utzon. After he had left Sydney in 1966, Utzon wrote to Arup pointing to the meeting with Ryan as 'a deliberate destruction of my – the architect's – position and possibilities to finalize the building.' Utzon understood from Ryan that Arup had 'demanded a new contract according to which I was supposed to be designer only, subordinate to the engineer.' This interpretation of the meeting contradicts all the written notes concerning the Arup proposals. Either Ryan misinterpreted Arup's suggestions, had forgotten the details (he related the story to Utzon four years after it took place) or Utzon misinterpreted Ryan's story.

It is certainly feasible, however, that Arup communicated some of his misgivings about Utzon's administrative capabilities. He wrote to Lewis on 24 September 1963: 'I am very fond of Jørn, he is inspiring company, and I consider him to be just about the best architect I have come across. But he also has some defects which his genius and lively imagination probably make unavoidable. Being an aesthete and an aristocrat he is inclined to value inspiring vision more than pedantic truth.'

Utzon much preferred the idea of reporting to SOHEC rather than the Public Works Department (PWD). The committee was generally sympathetic to his proposals, they believed him when he said, 'I have solved the problems', and they paid him when he asked for money. He did not want to give up this cosy relationship. Zunz wrote to Lewis in September 1963: 'There is no doubt in our minds where the real power lies and I think if Utzon persists in bluffing himself that it lies with the committee, it will merely complicate his, and unfortunately, our, lives.'

It was just then that SOHEC dropped its biggest bombshell that was to have major ramifications, not only for Utzon, but for the architects that would succeed him.

Utzon had been working on plans for the Major Hall that would provide for 2,800 seats, with 1,800 in front of the orchestra and 1,000 behind. Sir Charles Moses announced that this was unacceptable, largely because the seats behind the orchestra would be almost impossible to sell.

In the Red Book, Utzon had shown three arrangements for the hall – in opera mode showing the location of the moveable stage machinery, and in two layouts for concerts. One layout showed the orchestra in the middle with the audience on both sides and temporary seating on the stage; the other showed the orchestra at the south end. Following tests, it was found that the latter arrangement did not work because of the length of the hall and because the stage portal, as Utzon told Sir Bernard Heinze, 'virtually cut the hall in two' acoustically.

Utzon started developing the layout of the Major Hall in concert mode with the audience on both sides of the orchestra in 1961; SOHEC made no negative comments at the time.

The alarm was sounded by Charles Buttrose, Director of Publicity and Concerts at the ABC, whose main concern was the sale of seats. Also, Sir Bernard Heinze had just been on a tour of Europe where he had visited various concert halls, in particular Scharoun's Philharmonie which was nearing completion. He was unhappy about the idea of too large a number of seats behind the orchestra because so many concerts included soloists whose sound would not carry well to those seats. Heinze was, however, very impressed by the Philharmonie, 'A triumph of architectural design', and he wrote to Stan Haviland in September 1963 to say that he believed it to be 'of the utmost importance that we should have an objective opinion of the success or otherwise of the Berlin Philharmonic Hall.'

Cremer and Gabler were also against too many seats behind the orchestra. They advised that the proposed layout was particularly unsuitable for directional instruments and voice.

The news of changes to Utzon's proposals reached London in October 1963 when Lewis wrote to Zunz to report that Moses had recently voiced '…strong criticism of the proposal to accommodate 900 seats "behind" the orchestra in the Major Hall. This has resulted in a major planning change to the seating in this hall and obviously changes all the previous scheming for the auditorium ceiling (it was pretty nebulous anyway). The seating will be raised 7ft [2.1m] above the concrete steps and we will probably have to provide structural support by timber framing supported on steel or concrete girders. This is still at an early stage of development and is hot off the press. As soon as we receive Utzon's sketches (promised two weeks hence!) we will forward them to you.'

The only way to accommodate an extra 1,000 people in front of the orchestra was to widen the auditorium by cantilevering the seats over the side stairs, create a much steeper rake and to put the seating into three tiers instead of one. Utzon was also forced to reduce the row spacing from 3ft (914mm) to 2ft 10in (863mm) and 2ft 7in (788mm) – which, Lewis commented to Zunz, 'will affect our long legged friends.'

The Technical Advisory Panel accepted these alterations in November 1963, although it is not certain they understood the implications of the redesign. The minutes recorded that:

'This latest suggestion for reconstruction of the seating arrangements is the result of a continued effort on the part of the Architect to produce the best possible Concert Hall in accordance with the original requirements of the competition.

'This combination of widening the auditorium and "closing up" the seating rows enables the audience capacity to be provided within a much less depth than in the previous scheme.

'The Opera House Music and Drama Panel are completely satisfied with the suggestion and have pointed out there will be considerable reduction in running costs over the original scheme contemplated. There would appear to be no serious disadvantages associated with the change.'

What the Panel did not realize, however, was that the new seating layout would mean that the design work done to date on the ceilings for the Major Hall would have to be scrapped. The introduction of the tiers had reduced the reverberation time within the hall to unacceptable levels and both Cremer and Gabler were deeply unhappy.

One of the most fundamental changes brought about by the rearrangement of seats was that the Major Hall changed from being a convertible hall, which could be adjusted acoustically to take into account the different requirements of opera and concerts by varying the volume of the room using ceiling panels, into a multi-purpose hall with little or no ability to alter the air volume or the number of seats. The problem of the multi-purpose hall is that if you manage to increase the number of seats for concert use, the reverberation time becomes shorter – just the opposite of what you want to achieve.

However, the programme was forcing Utzon into accepting solutions that were less than perfect. The podium was built and the shells were under way – he had to work within constraints created by the partly finished building. The proposals for the tiered seating lacked the integrity of the previous structural work. At the time, Kelman described it as the 'sort of alteration one does when renovating an old theatre'. Lewis wrote to Zunz that it was 'structurally feasible but extremely inelegant'.

The beauty of the original Opera House design was the simplicity of Utzon's concept of the podium, shaped to create the two amphitheatres, with the roofs floating cloud-like above. Now a new piece of structure was to be shoehorned into the space, compromising the integrity of the scheme that Utzon had worked so hard for so long to maintain.

Zunz wrote to Lewis at the end of November saying that the proposals 'make us feel full of doom and despondency'. He wryly drew a parallel with the double skin roof proposal that had been rejected by Utzon in 1961. 'It was fundamentally the quickest and cheapest way of erecting the roof but was, and I think quite rightly, rejected because it was entirely out of character with the underlying concepts of the scheme.'

A remarkable exchange of letters in early 1964 that highlights the growing rift between Arup and Utzon begins with Arup saying how sorry he was to see the rearrangement of the concert hall and the steel structure above the concrete seating banks. 'I imagine you would not have agreed to this unless it was absolutely necessary, for I do not think you would have agreed to a solution which bears the marks of a compromise, and which seems to destroy some of the wonderful clarity and simplicity which characterized the original idea.'

Arup saw the development as a 'symbol of the shipwreck which our working together has suffered'. Writing in Danish, he said that, even before Utzon's departure to Sydney, he had the feeling that there was a danger he would be recruited into the 'Balslev Brigade' – a jokey reference used by members of the Opera House team to describe consultants who had fallen by the wayside. Balslev were the first team of electrical consultants and were pressed to resign by Utzon directly after the architect complained about their 'unusable' tender material for the Opera House lifts and the 'amateurish' treatment of the stage lighting.

To Arup it was clear that Utzon no longer needed him and he refers to his desire to restructure the contractual relationship:

'I must admit I was deeply affected by your attitude to my suggestion that clear lines were needed as regards the other engineering works. It had nothing to do with avarice, but on the contrary with the sound principle that responsibility and the right to make decisions must follow each other.

'Our people in Sydney are despondent, they do not feel there is progress with Stage 3, and they are fighting with great problems on Stage 2. I do not know whether you have thought of getting other engineers to help you with Stage 3 – that would in a way take quite a weight off our shoulders, but I do not think it is a realistic solution even if I would welcome the idea of someone else solving the problems and experiencing your method of working. And it would be a calamity politically – it is my opinion that it is unthinkable. We must therefore work together, there is no alternative.'

Utzon replied:

'Dear Ove, please desist from your criticism! Be secure in the knowledge that I am the only one who can manage Stage 3 of the project.

'Your criticism of me and your letter to M Lewis with your suggestion for the management of Stage 3 is wide of the mark. You have confused your staff and removed some of the respect for me on the part of M Lewis which is a precondition for us working together. Without knowing me or my staff he has indicated that he has doubts about our management skills. That I can only regard as being the result of the attitude of his boss, which is you. Management is in a way the easiest part of the job, something which most people can learn. The difficult part, the real problem is to create the possibility of achieving what you want, and that, you must admit, I have shown myself able to master.'

Later in the year, Arup became so concerned with his firm's relationship that he and Zunz travelled to Sydney to suggest to Utzon that they withdraw from the final phase of the project. The minutes of the Technical Advisory Panel on 5 May 1966, after Utzon resigned, record that, 'Mr Arup went as far as to mention that during his last visit to Sydney some eighteen months ago he had informed Mr Utzon of his firm's intention to resign from the Stage 3 contract because of the lack of collaboration but on Mr Utzon's request and after considerable discussion with him, decided against this course.'

However, as the problems with the seating showed, Utzon was finding it more and more difficult to achieve what he wanted. Circumstances were compromising perfection. In his book *Utzon and the Sydney Opera House – A Statement in the Public Interest*, Elias Duek-Cohen argued that the closed up seating with back-to-back spacing of 2ft 7in (788mm) and 2ft 5in (704mm) was perfectly acceptable since this had been employed in recent European concert halls such as London's Festival Hall, which had a spacing of 2ft 7in (788mm). He was correct as far as the larger measurement was concerned. The Greater London Council Places of Public Entertainment Technical Regulations required that the seating area assigned to each person should not be less than 2ft 6in (760mm). Duek-Cohen also suggested that the design of the seats would be thinner than conventional seats thus making the space seem more generous. While this solution may have been workable, it did not meet Utzon's own requirement for the perfect opera house. He had already provided 3ft (915mm) spacing in the less problematic Minor Hall, so one might assume that this would have been his preferred measurement.

The problems created by Moses' decision to eliminate the audience from behind the orchestra seemed to be the culmination of a series of misunderstandings and an apparent lack of communication between Utzon and SOHEC, and between Utzon and his consultants.

After the departure of the architect, SOHEC (by then called the Sydney Opera House Trust) issued a public statement:

'The conditions for the International competition stipulated that the large hall should seat between 3,000 and 3,500 persons. The sketch plans of the winning design submitted by Mr Jørn Utzon did not indicate the detailed seating accommodation, but upon appointment as Architect he was informed by letter of 8 November 1957 that the main hall should provide for 3,000 persons. The drawings submitted by him in March 1958 were approved in principle by the Executive Committee on the advice of its Technical and Music and Drama Panels but certain amendments were required. Fresh drawings embodying these amendments were prepared by the Architect in June of that year. These provided for 2,800 seats for concerts, 3ft between rows and seats 22ins [558mm] wide. In November 1963 the Architect submitted a proposal for some of the audience to be seated behind the orchestra but the Committee rejected it.

'In the meantime special circumstances relating to the ceiling structure and acoustics called for attention. The architect reported progress on each of these aspects. Each report continued to refer to the 2,800 seating capacity. There were two lengthy reports in 1965, also a verbal report in February this year. Not once did he indicate that seat dimensions were being changed in this way.'

The committee did not see their rejection of the idea of seating some of the audience behind the orchestra as a 'change of mind', despite the fact that it appeared in the Red Book of 1958 as one of the two options for the layout of the concert hall; the arrangement is also clearly shown in drawings of 1960 which show the orchestra placed at one third of the length of the hall.

Bill Wheatland, Utzon's assistant, was of the view that SOHEC had accepted the principle of the audience behind the orchestra when it agreed to the purchase of the stage machinery, which implied that the orchestra would be placed towards the centre of the hall.

Members of the committee clearly did not fully understand the minutes of the Technical Advisory Panel, meeting number 45 held on 18 November 1963, or worked out what 'closing up' the seating rows really meant.

Yuzo Mikami in his book, *Utzon's Sphere*, suggests that Utzon should have stood firm against Moses since, within the constraints created by the building, a convertible hall was the only way to meet the three main requirements for the concert hall: to provide 2,800 comfortable seats; to attain an air volume of approximately 1 million cu ft (28,000 cu m) needed for a reverberation time of 2 seconds; and to plan all the seats within a maximum distance of 115ft–130ft (35m–40m) from the orchestra podium.

The problem was that Utzon was getting conflicting advice and communications were poor. He was dealing with three acoustics consultants – the Danish Jordan and two Germans, Cremer and Gabler – complicated by the fact that Cremer, although he could speak English, would only write his reports in German. To make matters worse, Jordan did not agree with Cremer and Gabler in their overall approach; he preferred the classic 'shoe-box' style of auditorium, which he had recommended in the Red Book, while the Germans were more adventurous in their approach to the shape of the auditoria. Although the brief had clearly set out that concert use was to be given priority over opera, when Cremer and Gabler started work they were presented with an 'opera house'; it was called an 'opera house' and it was to be fitted with extensive stage machinery as an opera house should be. As Utzon amended the design of the hall from a single space with a faceted ceiling to a theatre layout with a fixed proscenium and radiating ceiling, it became more and more like a space where the priority was opera.

Writing about the Opera House later in his book *Acoustical Design in Concert Halls and Theatres*, Jordan wrote: 'The name opera house conveyed the impression of prestige and vanity and dominated the legitimate aspiration of friends of musical life in Sydney – a good modern concert hall to be the home of the Sydney Symphony Orchestra.' He described Utzon's designs as 'original to the point of being revolutionary, but which, unfortunately, had absolutely no association with the classical design of concert halls'. On his relationship with Cremer and Gabler, he wrote: 'Over a few years the situation concerning acoustic consultancy had developed from a simple request of wanting a second opinion to the ambiguity of uncertain responsibilities, and missed opportunities of co-operation between the parties involved.'

The problem of the building's title is significant. In an article in *Walkabout* magazine in 1961, Sir Charles Moses wrote: 'The Sydney Opera House is misnamed. It is not an Opera House. It is a group of four halls of varying sizes, in two of which opera could be presented from time to time, perhaps for a total of eight weeks each year.' The comment is particularly ironic in light of the fact that, at the time of Utzon's departure, it was members of staff at the ABC who were concerned that the hall had been modified so far in the direction of conventional opera/theatre design that it would be unsuitable for use by the Sydney Symphony Orchestra.

Following SOHEC's decision to reject the layout with the audience on both sides of the orchestra, Utzon was finding it difficult to progress with the design of the Major Hall ceiling and he wrote to Cremer on 10 December 1963: 'We are approaching the stage where a constant close co-operation with the consultants will be required until everything is decided upon, I feel that the best way this can be done is through direct co-operation in my office in Sydney.' It was suggested that Joachim Nutsch from Cremer's office should visit Sydney for around two months. However, Nutsch did not arrive in Sydney until April 1964, which meant that the architects were unable to progress work on the ceilings for six months.

Nutsch stayed for six weeks and, in that time, developed the designs for the Minor Hall so that it was 'acoustically functional'. But he struggled to solve the problems of the Major Hall – the search for a solution was hampered by the fact that the Utzon office was working from incorrect drawings. In November 1963, they had completed drawing SOH 1040; copying an Arups drawing that illustrated the 8ft (2.44m) clearance line for services, they mistook this for the internal profile of the shells, thus hugely reducing the available volume of the Major Hall. The error was not discovered until January 1966.

It comes as little surprise that Lewis was not getting the drawings he required, particularly as, at the same time, Utzon was preparing his invited entry for the Zurich Schauspielhaus competition, which he duly won in May 1964. He also entered the Madrid National Opera competition, but was unplaced. In his published letters to his parents, Prip-Buus writes on 30 May 1964, 'After he [Jørn] left, we finished the competition submission he had been invited to do for the theatre in Zurich. It is something I have been working on for the last couple of months and one of the reasons for my being so busy – the [Silkeborg] museum, this and normal work.'

In March 1964, a frustrated Lewis had written to Zunz regarding the auditorium ceilings saying that Utzon had been telling him for nine months that he could expect drawings in 'three weeks' time'. He was worried that the administration and preparation of documents were being 'hopelessly mishandled'.

In April he repeated his complaint about the non-delivery of drawings. 'On 1.10.63 we were told that modifications to the Major Hall seating would be sent in two weeks and the Minor Hall in three weeks. To date we have received nothing on the Minor Hall and a preliminary scheme for the seating of the Major Hall.'

Lewis was becoming concerned at the ability of Utzon's team to physically produce the work. He had extracted various costs from Utzon to present to the Minister and commented to Zunz, 'I leave it to your judgement whether you think he can produce the documents for roughly A£4m worth of work with a staff of two administrative architects and seven design architects.'

Lewis reported that Utzon had estimated a completion date for the Opera House of February 1967 – a date selected without any reference either to Arups or to Hornibrook.

Relations between architect and engineer had not improved. Lewis continued, 'Utzon persistently refuses to allow us to enter his office through the back door.'

Progress was slow. Lewis had written to Zunz in March providing a detailed breakdown of the situation. Lewis said that he had been asking for information on the glass walls from April to August 1963 in order to proceed with the engineering drawings. Then in October he was told that Miller Milston and Ferris, Symonds' engineers, could solve all the problems, leaving Arups less to do. 'Our design meetings and analysis over a period of two and a half months have brought forward only one significant conclusion – namely that Symonds and their consulting engineers have not made any advance on the engineering problems of the glass walls nor will any of the tests they have done in the past be at all useful.'

By March 1964, Lewis had received nothing on the Major Hall and only a preliminary scheme for the Minor Hall. But Lewis was not the only one finding it difficult to establish what was going on in Utzon's office. The Government, concerned at the lack of progress and rising costs, appointed a liaison architect on 5 March 1964 to provide a link between Utzon and the PWD. Bill Wood was a supervising architect from the department who was nearing retirement. In his diaries, Prip-Buus describes Wood, '...an old architect from Public Works has been foisted on us to keep a check on us.'

Utzon was none too pleased and wrote to the Director of Public Works: 'I myself and my staff will do everything to assist Mr Wood in becoming familiar with the plans and proceedings of the Opera House, but I have to state that as I am appointed the Architect, I cannot let Mr Wood interfere in the administration of the scheme or allow him access to drawings and documents in my office.' In Utzon's view, Wood was only a carrier of information from his office to the Minister's. In an interview in 1980 Ted Farmer, the Government architect in the 1960s described how the Director of the PWD 'got one of my staff and put them in as a sort of spy down there to see if he could find out what was going on'.

Utzon's reply did not please Minister Ryan who called him in on 16 June to discuss the increase of costs from A£12.5million to A£17.4million. Stating he was 'disappointed' at the tone of the letter, the Minister said that Wood represented him and he would expect him to be taken into consultation at all times on all matters affecting the design and construction of the Opera House. Utzon 'expressed regret that there had been a misunderstanding,' and said that he would do what he could to ensure that such a situation did not reoccur.

The Minister stressed that the Sydney Opera House was a public work and that his departmental officers must be recognized as those who would administer the project. He also made it clear that he was the constructing authority and that SOHEC was advisory to him.

However, Utzon was never happy with Wood. Wood was an administrative architect and not a designer; he was definitely not on Utzon's wavelength. Lewis suggests he was 'baffled' by Utzon.

On 17 July, the Government released a statement in which it declared that costs were to be restricted to A£12.5millon and that the architect should look at reducing the costs to that amount. It was announced that work would not proceed on Stage 3 until the architect had provided a detailed report on the proposals and 'prepared working drawings and documents required for competitive tenders (except in a few places as approved by the Minister).'

Soon afterwards, Lewis told Utzon that the only way to satisfy the Minister's condition would be to set up a drawing office working almost independently of the architect, but maintain sufficient liaison to fulfil the design requirements. Utzon did not like this suggestion. He said that it had been tried without success by Corbusier, Mies van der Rohe, Alvar Aalto and Frank Lloyd Wright.

On 23 July, Utzon met with the Premier and a Cabinet sub-committee that had been formed to look into the administration of the Opera House. Lewis wrote to London the same day. 'I have just returned from a most unpleasant interview with the Premier and various ministers – Hills [Local Government], Ryan [Public Works] and Compton [Agriculture].' Utzon was given a mauling over the increase in costs and unwisely raised the question of car parking provision near the Opera House, something he had been asked to investigate by SOHEC, but which was news to Hills who was in charge of the development of the Circular Quay area. Utzon was then subjected to what Lewis describes as 'pretty abusive' treatment by Hills and was told to stick to the design of the building itself and not to tinker with areas that did not concern him.

Utzon pleaded for the reinstatement of SOHEC as client, and was told in no uncertain terms that its role would be purely advisory in future.

The project was also becoming embroiled in wider politics. Elections were looming and the Opera House was an issue. The Liberal Party opposition had got wind of the fact that costs were rising close to A£18million. The newspapers picked up on the increases and had a field day.

Various issues were worrying the Minister – there had been no information on the acoustic treatment or the seating arrangements of the Major Hall, and he was unwilling to go back to Parliament to request an increase in expenditure so asked Utzon to look again at the costs. The department was also concerned at 'irresponsible statements made by some people' (believed to be Ashworth) that cost was not a significant factor in the project. 'This is completely untrue; this is expenditure of public moneys and cost is of the utmost importance.'

The pressures were beginning to take their toll. In his July letter to his parents, Prip-Buus raises the issue of resignation should the architects have to water down the designs. 'We will finish the designs and then if they won't build on the basis of them, we must leave, as we have no intention of ruining the opera house by going along with compromises.'

In the aftermath of Utzon's departure, it was often suggested that it was Davis Hughes who hounded Utzon out of the job, but it was Ryan who set the ball rolling. The fact that, once he was in opposition, Ryan became an ally of Utzon was interpreted by him as a change of heart, whereas it was more a reflection of the highly adversarial nature of Australian politics. During the state elections campaign in 1968, the Labor Party did not promise to bring Utzon back if they won.

CHAPTER 5
THE TURN OF THE SCREW

In August 1964, Utzon visited Zurich for the Schauspielhaus project and then Berlin to confer with Cremer. On his way back to Sydney he stopped off in London to meet with Zunz and Arup. In a plain-speaking meeting with 'occasional banging of fists', Utzon sought the London office's support in his shaky relationship with Lewis and his team.

Afterwards Zunz wrote to Lewis: 'He is nettled at the thought of our not supporting him in handling Stage 3. He put up very powerful arguments to support his case and insists …we support him loyally as he has supported us in Stages 1 and 2. We should do this.' It was important that the two teams should show a united front 'provided it does not conflict with our basic responsibilities to the client,' Zunz continued.

Utzon was particularly keen to arrange a negotiated contract on the supply of various plywood elements for Stage 3 – in particular the auditoria ceilings, rehearsal room interiors, corridor panelling and the glass wall mullions. The Government did not like negotiated contracts, preferring them to go out to tender; negotiated contracts laid them open to criticism from disappointed suppliers and could be misinterpreted.

Utzon had told Zunz that he was quite willing to agree with the Premier's demand for firm tenders where possible, but that he would have to advise him that the job would consequently be delayed. However, Zunz wrote, 'there is no doubt a strong basis for the argument that with some suppliers he should be given powers to negotiate.'

The Labor Government had, however, agreed to a negotiated contract with Hornibrook for Stage 2, and entered a management contract with them when it was clear that there was not enough information on which contractors would tender, but to wait for sufficient information would have led to an unacceptable increase in the programme. With hindsight it would have been sensible for Stage 1 to have been a negotiated contract since it was commenced with very little information on which the tenderers could calculate their price accurately.

The ability to nominate subcontractors was important if Utzon was going to be able to develop his radical designs for the auditoria ceilings and the glass walls. As with tile-makers Hoganas, he liked to develop products in conjunction with the manufacturer.

For the plywood work in Stage 3, Utzon wished to appoint Ralph Symonds Limited, who were world leaders in plywood technology and could do things with the material that no other company could. The factory was able to produce massive 49ft x 9ft (15m x 2.7m) sheets compared to the industry standard of 8ft x 4ft 6in (2.4m x 1.4m). They could bond metal sheet to ply either in the form of a sandwich or as a weatherproof coating.

Symonds had made contact with Utzon when the company was producing the formwork for Stage 1 and Utzon had been so excited by the possibilities of the material that he started to design a plywood house for himself. He based the whole concept of the auditoria ceilings on Symonds' ability to make large sheets that could be reinforced structurally with integral metal sheeting. Utzon described the construction of the ceilings as 'basically similar to boats'. He proposed huge beams that would span from the back of the auditorium to the proscenium, delivered to the site in one piece.

It was an important part of the design process for Utzon to be able to build full-size mock-ups of the ceilings and the window mullions. Symonds had made some smaller prototypes with money authorized by Ryan, but the situation had reached a stage where Symonds would do no more without a contract.

The Technical Advisory Panel produced a report which stated strongly that Symonds should be nominated. If they were not, the ceilings would have to be redesigned because other manufacturers could only produce small sheets that would have to be scarfed together, and all the work carried out to date would be wasted. However, the Panel did not cut much ice with the PWD, who insisted on competitive tenders and even suggested that Symonds should make the work done to date available to competitors who might wish to tender.

By August 1964, Utzon had refined the ceiling of the Minor Hall to the extent that he was ready to build a prototype of the huge U-shaped beams that would form the radiating structure. Ryan refused to sanction the mock-ups, partly because it would jeopardize the principle of competitive public tendering, but also because Symonds had gone into receivership in February 1964.

This would have posed a major problem for Hornibrook. Symonds would have been, in effect, their subcontractor and director Corbet Gore was not happy to be working with a firm that was in receivership on such a large contract. Through their bankers, Symonds offered a bond of A£50,000, but Gore felt that to be inadequate. He told the Opera House Oral History project: 'The contract would have been worth several millions, and to give that sort of contract to a bloke in receivership – what am I going to do if we're left in the lurch and he can't finish? Fifty thousand wouldn't have got me out of trouble.'

The inability to progress with the prototypes brought work in the Utzon office on site almost to a standstill and three of the staff resigned because there was so little to do.

In November, Utzon opened an office at Palm Beach, some way from the centre of Sydney. He was hoping to recreate some of the peace and calm of his Hellebæk office. Prip-Buus wrote home to say: 'We have got a new studio, out in Palm Beach, an old boatbuilder's yard right down by Pittwater. There is simply never any peace in the Opera House, so we needed to find a place where people are not coming all the time, and where there is no phone, so now a couple of us are out here with Jørn, sketching (plus designing for the Zurich project), and then Jørn and I are in town Mondays and Thursdays for meetings and to give instructions for the final designs there. It's almost like being in Hellebæk again.'

On the subject of drawings he writes, 'We are forced to rein in because we can't go on until we have information on various firms that are to do the work.'

At the end of October 1964, a rift developed between Utzon and the NSW Chapter of the Royal Australian Institute of Architects (RAIA) that was to have serious implications at the time of Utzon's departure. Public relations on the Opera House were very poor; the PWD did not like anyone involved in the project, except themselves, to speak to the press. In August, SOHEC discussed the problem. Haviland said that he had received an edict from the PWD to say that all public relations should be channelled through the department. Sir Bernard Heinze complained that the Minister was not a public relations expert and that 'the present atmosphere had arisen through ineffective public relations being established.'

There was continual criticism of the project in the media and the RAIA was worried that this negative comment was bad for the profession. Ron Gilling, the president of the NSW Chapter, wrote to Premier J B Renshaw suggesting that the RAIA should co-operate on the publication of a report outlining the various aspects of the project:

'Naturally many architects are asked,' wrote Gilling on 30 October 1964, 'both publicly and privately, for their comments and opinions on the Opera House, particularly in regard to construction and cost. Many find it impossible to continue to reply with "no comment", but this reply is almost forced upon this profession because of the lack of general information on the whole project.

'I assure you that our desire is to help. The Sydney Opera House is far from finished and will no doubt be the subject of wide criticism from time to time. This, we feel, should be avoided and we are willing to do our part to achieve the most advantageous result for a great building, which is now firmly focused in the eyes of the world.'

Gilling suggested that the Chapter should collaborate to produce a report on the state of the project. He proposed a committee of members from SOHEC, the PWD and two architects from the Chapter to assist Utzon to produce a report that would be aimed specifically at the architectural profession.

The proposal was referred by the Premier's office to Utzon and to SOHEC, neither of whom were in favour. Utzon suggested that the only possible way of dealing with public relations was 'through one body, which is the Minister for Public Works'. The RAIA took the proposal no further, but Utzon saw the institute's action as an unwarranted intrusion into his affairs.

Another event that increased Utzon's feelings of defensiveness was a report on the shell structures that Minister Ryan requested from the engineers in November. Utzon was annoyed that Ryan had asked for the report direct from Arups, and they had replied without going through him. Nor did he like the fact that the report discussed the design totally from the engineers' point of view and did not give him sufficient credit in the design process.

It has been one of the contentions of the Utzon team that their opponents never understood their method of working, where the architects would provide design drawings and the subcontractors would do the 'shop' drawings that would provide sufficient data for the various elements to be made. They were clearly unable to communicate their methodology to the rest of the team. At a meeting with the PWD on 20 January 1965, Corbet Gore told the department that, in his opinion, the architect did not have any working drawings, specifications or any other details to enable any part of Stage 3 to go to tender. Gore added, 'Whilst the Architect is certain when he sees the material or finish that he wants, he does not seem to be able to specify this beforehand.'

Arups could not understand why Utzon's working methods should mean they could not be supplied with drawings. Other architects the firm had worked with also insisted on prototypes, but they were always backed up by the usual specification and drawing procedures.

Ryan was becoming increasingly agitated. On 26 January 1965, he called Utzon in to his office and gave him a stern dressing down:

'It is nearly 12 months since you submitted to me what was purported to be an up-to-date report on the cost of the Opera House ...I understood that it was clearly understood by you what the [Cabinet Sub-] Committee's requirements were in relation to a detailed explanation of all the remaining work involved... We confidently anticipated that those requests would have been long since met by you but the present position is that we are no further ahead with the detailed explanation... None of the information is adequate nor does it nearly approach what is required and for that reason I am very very disturbed because this job cannot proceed until such time as this information is supplied... You have indicated to me several times that you understand and appreciate this problem but up to the present time there is no evidence forthcoming to substantiate your statement. The Cabinet Sub-Committee's request was clear and specific and it has not been complied with... We have no completed drawings for Stage 3. We agreed we would have bimonthly reports on all these matters. They have not been forthcoming...'

Utzon responded in his usual confident fashion, a manner which, in the past, had convinced SOHEC: '...there is nothing wrong. You and your Government should be happy and proud of what takes place down there. This is because we have strived to make this building perfect on all points.'

In an increasingly testy exchange the Minister attempted to pin Utzon down:

Minister: What working drawings for Stage 3 have you completed?

Mr Utzon: I have working drawings for several parts of Stage 3.

Minister: Why haven't you submitted that detail to me?

Mr Utzon:	Because I haven't got the final working drawings.
Minister:	But why haven't you told me that?
Mr Utzon:	It is obvious from our schedules. I have delivered reports which are on schedules which clearly show the stages of progress.

Then:

Mr Johnson	(Director of Public Works): Stage 3 will involve a lot of tendering and this can only be done on the basis of working drawings.
Mr Utzon:	We want Hornibrook in on Stage 3. The contractor must come in on the design period.
Minister:	We accept that. There is no argument on that score.
Mr Johnson:	We are depending on you to give us the information before we can authorise it.

Later:

Minister:	Do you think the Cabinet set up a Sub-Committee for fun? Do you think you can talk to them and forget about it? From the point of view of administration there has been a lack of co-operation by you. These letters have been written to you and they haven't been answered. Now you tell me you haven't the full information. Until such time as I have the information I am not going to make a decision on the completion of Phase 3.

As a result of the meeting, Utzon produced, a week later, a 'Descriptive Narrative' that set out the current position on the design. In it, Utzon said that the design could not be developed to finality until further prototypes were made. 'Ralph Symonds will not make their know-how or equipment available for hot-bonding large sheets of plywood unless they have some assurance of being nominated sub-contractors.'

In response to the Narrative, Wood wrote to the Secretary and Director of Public Works on 22 February:

'It is abundantly evident that a vast amount of work remains to be done in the form of dimensioned and working drawings and specifications. The information contained in the narrative description is interesting and enlightening but totally inadequate to permit the quantity surveyors to make more than an approximate estimate of cost. In order to prepare the necessary drawings and other data the Architect needs a staff of some 30 persons to cope with the situation.'

Despite the Minister's hard talking at the beginning of the year, there was a sense of hiatus as the May election loomed. Ryan seemed happy to sweep the Opera House under the carpet for the moment while he was busy on the stump.

Meanwhile, Arups were attempting to keep the ball rolling on the design of the interiors. The minutes of the weekly meeting on 1 March 1965 between the engineers (Lewis and Nutt) and the architects (Wheatland and Maclurcan) make grim reading:

Major Hall – ceilings – information awaited from architect.

Major Hall – balconies – architect's drawings awaited.

Major Hall – galleries – The engineer stated a clear preference for precast seating – Architect's opinion awaited.

Levels – awaited from architect.

Major Hall – seating – Engineer's scheme under consideration by the Architect.

Ceiling suspension – Engineer's scheme under consideration by the Architect.

Thickness of Plywood Web Members – the Architect reported that all items listed under 5.3 were the subject of a letter to the acoustics consultants, in which it also requested that Dr Nutsch be brought to Australia as soon as possible to assist in resolving these problems.

Finish of the rear walls of Major Hall – Information Required from Architect.

And so it continued in the same vein covering glass walls, cladding and paving.

Utzon's office was grinding to a halt. Two of the most experienced staff were about to leave. Jon Lundberg was planning to return to Denmark, as was Skipper Nielsen, who had been working on the project since 1960, Jacob Keilland-Brandt was seriously ill and in May had to go back to Denmark for an operation. Utzon's office records show that he had nine architects working in the Sydney office at the end of 1965; he took on more architects to replace those who resigned and a further three by the end of November providing a complement of 12. For all of them it was their first experience of a major building project.

On 1 July, there was a meeting at the architect's office that illustrated just how far the working relationship between engineer and architect had shifted from Ove Arup's ideal of 'total architecture'. Lewis asked if it was possible for the engineers to follow the architect's development of the scheme while drawings were being prepared instead of waiting until they were presented with the finished piece. Utzon explained that he 'could not allow any disturbance in the drawing office and it was necessary to work undisturbed during the development of his ideas and systems as the scheme could suffer by side-tracking at that stage'. In the margin of the copy of the minutes sent to London, Lewis remarked, 'This just about sums the relationship up.'

However, matters were about to take a very different course. On 1 May 1965, the Labor Party was defeated in the polls and a coalition of the Liberal and Country Parties took over under the Premiership of Robert W Askin. The Liberal Party's supporters were largely from the cities and subsidizing a project like the Opera House might be seen as favouring this constituency. Askin thought it was better politically that the Opera House was overseen by a member of the Country Party, which had traditionally been critical of public expenditure on effete cultural projects, particularly at a time when country areas were being devastated by drought. So he appointed Davis Hughes, the Country Party member for the rural constituency of Armidale and a tough, plain-speaking politician, to take over the Public Works portfolio including the Opera House. Utzon's team hoped that things would improve – at least nothing could be worse than the situation under Labor.

Things started well. Following Utzon's meeting with Davis Hughes on 16 June, Prip-Buus wrote: '…if the prospects are not entirely rosy for us, at least the new people will appreciate our work and help us to get it finished instead of opposing us and putting spokes in our wheel like the last lot did. We'll see, but everything suggests a change that in our eyes is almost a miracle after the experiences of the last few years.'

But Prip-Buus' optimism was premature. During the election the Liberals had promised to sort out the Opera House and put its organization onto a business-like footing. Davis Hughes lost no time in carrying out the election promises. Prip-Buus' diary entry of 31 August 1965 reports that, '…we are at the moment going through the worst crisis in the history of the project.'

Earlier in the month, Wood had reported to the new Minister on how the project might be controlled in the future. One of the proposals that caused much consternation in the Utzon camp was the suggestion that the department could control the architect by withholding fees or instructing SOHEC or the SOH Trust to do so. 'This I have always termed "cheque book control" and no other method is equally efficacious,' wrote Wood. He had proposed such a strategy to Ryan, but nothing had come of it.

In the past, SOHEC had been willing to pass payment to Utzon whenever he requested. Now they would only be permitted to pay him when it could be shown that he had carried out particular pieces of work.

Wood's report also suggested that the Government set down a maximum figure within which the Opera House must be completed. He prepared a list of 44 subcontracts that could all be allocated costs and proposed that a critical path analysis of Stage 3 should be immediately prepared that integrated the schedules of the architect and the consultants.

'It is very doubtful,' wrote Wood, 'whether Mr Utzon has or foresees the engagement of a staff adequate to meet the needs of this gigantic project.' He proposed that the department authorize the setting up of a drafting office or subcontracting the work to an outside firm. Some 25 architects, assistant architects and architectural assistants, together with a senior department architect, would be needed. 'These would have to be controlled independently of the Contractor, and in collaboration with Mr Utzon.'

He suggested that these proposals should be communicated in a 'firm but amicable' manner. 'To replace him as the designer would present serious difficulties and would cause a scandal with worldwide reverberations,' he stated presciently.

The issues raised by Wood with regard to staffing led to a meeting which was viewed by Utzon as a betrayal by the local architectural establishment. Ron Gilling was invited to lunch with Davis Hughes. At the time of the invitation no mention was made of the subject matter of the meeting. When they met, the Minister began by asking Gilling a number of questions about the rights of a client, without mentioning the Opera House, although Gilling says in his account of his role in the affair, 'only a fool would not have guessed what the Minister was driving at.'

Davis Hughes asked:

'As a client am I entitled to know how long a project will take?'

'Am I entitled to know how much it will cost?'

'Am I entitled to ask my architect to meet me on a regular basis?'

'Am I entitled to receive the working drawings?'

To each of these, Gilling responded 'Yes'.

Over lunch, the Minister explained some of his concerns on the progress of Stage 3. The previous month, the quantity surveyors had submitted a new estimate but had reported that they had been unable to obtain proper information to work from – they could only access 'preliminary and not working drawings'.

The Minister said that Utzon would not attend site meetings and he was concerned whether Utzon had sufficient staff to cope with the workload. Gilling told the Minister that, while there was full employment in the profession and draughtsmen were very scarce, if Utzon made an appeal for assistance 'the profession would rally round'.

After the lunch, Gilling telephoned Utzon to report the Minister's comment, but found that he was away and instead spoke to Robert Maclurcan, an architect in Utzon's office who also happened to be a member of the RAIA Chapter Council. Maclurcan so convinced Gilling that Utzon was on top of the job and that working drawings were well under way that Gilling suggested Maclurcan should meet with Davis Hughes to explain the situation to him. Utzon arrived back from holiday on 25 August, the day of the meeting, and was told about it by Maclurcan. Gilling thought that Maclurcan would be a preferable spokesman because he felt Utzon had a 'language problem'.

Unfortunately, when he met the Minister, Maclurcan was somewhat overawed by the situation and failed to be as convincing as he had previously been. The Minister did not feel he had received any satisfactory answers, particularly as Maclurcan gave the impression that the office was understaffed.

There was clearly a misunderstanding between Utzon and Gilling regarding Maclurcan's role. Gilling saw him as a representative of Utzon; however, Prip-Buus wrote to his parents that Maclurcan took part in the meeting 'not as our employee but as a member of the Association's Committee'.

Prip-Buus went on to say that Maclurcan claimed the meeting was confidential, and that he soothed the Minister by saying that the previous year, '…there was only one man working on the Opera House, while the rest were preparing the Zurich competition – (a fat lie based on jealousy) – but there were now 11 men occupied with the project, also a lie, as there are 16 of us in Sydney and three outside Australia.' However, Gilling says that the subject of Zurich was not mentioned in front of the Minister. Utzon was furious with Maclurcan and fired him. This was a rash move by Utzon as Maclurcan was his most experienced architect who had taken time out from his own practice to work with the Dane.

A month later, Gilling enjoyed an amicable lunch with Utzon and was given a guided tour of the site; at no time, says Gilling, did Utzon suggest he was unhappy about Gilling's meeting with the Minister. During the tour, Utzon made a telling comment saying that the Opera House could not be documented in the conventional manner. Gilling suggested that there must be a stage where he said 'build it'; Utzon's response was 'You are so naïve'. Utzon did not believe that Gilling could possibly understand his unconventional working methods. His retort sums up the impossibility of his relationship with the architectural establishment.

Following Wood's report, Davis Hughes sent an important minute to the Cabinet, dated 25 August 1965, setting out the current situation with Utzon. He announced that the latest (unpublished) estimate from Rider Hunt put the cost at A£24.2 million, however the quantity surveyors had added a caveat about the 'preliminary nature of the drawings' and the fact that they had not seen a comprehensive up-to-date works programme for Stage 3.

'Some of the Architect's proposals for Stage 3 must be fully examined as to structural questions, construction method, cost and alternatives, before approval is given to them proceeding as intended in the Architect's present design. Some of the matters to be reviewed with the Architect are:

'Mullions for suspended glass walls; the Architect proposes to construct these in laminated plywood covered externally in bronze. A great deal of experimental work is involved with no guarantee of ultimate success, and the cost factor is uncertain. Supply and erection is at present estimated at approximately £300,000.

'Proposed use of laminated timber trusses to support the plywood superstructure of the auditoria. There are structural considerations involved and other solutions may be preferable...'

Davis Hughes accepted that a substantial part of the plywood contract would have to be given to Symonds as they were the only company to have the necessary equipment to produce the ceiling beams; however, he raised concerns over the fact that the company was in receivership. He also told the Cabinet that closer controls and 'oversighting' of the architect were envisaged and that the Government would insist on proper working drawings and documents for tendering within a reasonable time. He foresaw that this would involve a considerable increase in the number of staff employed by Utzon or Utzon would have to let out some of the drawing work to a suitable firm of architects.

He also suggested that serious consideration should be given to renegotiating the architect's fee, which was originally settled when the costs of works stood at A£3.6 million:

'It is possible,' concluded Davis Hughes, 'that the action outlined above could lead to friction with the architect... It may be that the government will be faced with the architect not co-operating or, ultimately, wishing to withdraw from the project. While this would indeed be regrettable and have the most serious repercussions both local and international, there can be no justification for permitting the present unsatisfactory position as to preparation of drawings for Stage 3 to continue.'

The resignation of the architect was something that Davis Hughes was willing to contemplate in order to bring the contract under control. Neither he, nor indeed Wood, raised any issues regarding the deleterious effect such a course would have on the quality of the architecture and the integrity of the complete design – they worked to a different set of priorities.

Utzon was already threatening to react in just the way Davis Hughes had forecast. In a letter to the Minister written on 27 August, he complained that Davis Hughes did not fully understand his role on the project. Clearly stung by suggestions that the first two phases were perceived as largely engineering achievements, he complained, 'You obviously do not realize that everything that exists at Bennelong Point today I have been doing personally in my office. Every single piece of concrete has been completely designed and controlled by me.' He suggested that the Minister's lack of confidence might be restored if he had a meeting with SOHEC, 'my first client', with whom he had worked 'in complete harmony and with confidence', so that the committee could inform the Minister of the architect's qualifications.

'If you do not accept my way of working,' added Utzon, 'I am sorry but you will have to find another architect to carry out the rest of the job.'

Alarmed that they would get the blame for the increases in cost, the Government put out a press release at the end of August placing responsibility firmly at the door of their predecessors: '...there is no doubt that the previous Government allowed the costs to get out of hand.' However, it was hardly necessary to make a huge political issue out of the estimates because, despite the increases, the lottery income was keeping pace with costs. At the end of the tax year 1964/65, the Opera House account had a credit balance of A£5,151,288 and income for the year was A£2,979,847.

Davis Hughes' next turn of the screw was to institute Wood's stratagem of 'cheque book control'. PWD sent a letter to the Under Secretary and Controller of Accounts: 'All matters relating to accounts for the Sydney Opera House will now be the direct responsibility of the Department.' In future, instead of being paid by SOHEC as a formality, the architect would be paid according to the amount of work carried out. The delays that arose from this new system were soon to cause Utzon serious cash flow problems.

Cremer's assistant acoustic engineer, Nutsch, arrived in Sydney for a second time at the end of October and struggled to fit the required number of seats into the Major Hall. On 8 December, he reported to Cremer in Berlin that the capacity for concerts was 2,738. By January, this had dropped to 2,518, the reason being that new drawings had been done to ¼ scale, which allowed a more accurate layout than the ⅛ scale drawings that had been used to date. The only way to house the extra 300 people was behind the orchestra. Nutsch thought this less than ideal, particularly as Utzon's design for the Major Hall was now more like a theatre, with a proscenium cutting the space in two:

'Acoustically one gets a main room with an orchestra shell with a small room coupled onto it. 300 people sit in a most unfavourable position behind the orchestra. Because of the iron curtain …they are optically, as well as acoustically, totally divided from the main auditorium. Furthermore it is to be assumed that technical difficulties regarding access, stairs, air conditioning and lighting are at the present stage of construction not able to be accommodated. The expense of building this small room behind the orchestra would be immense.'

The iron curtain Nutsch refers to is the fire curtain that separates the audience from the stage area; when raised, this had to fit underneath the shell thus determining the height of the proscenium. Nutsch asked Cremer to write to Utzon explaining the situation. Cremer's response arrived ten days before Utzon resigned:

'Mr Nutsch wrote me that the number of seats in the Major Hall should be increased to 2800. …any addition of further seats would acoustically overload the hall. If you increase the number of seats in a given volume it is similar to increasing a barrel of wine by adding more water. You may fill more glasses but then everybody gets a worse wine.'

It is generally recognized that a hall of around 1,700 to 2,000 provides the ideal size for concerts. The Sydney Symphony Orchestra wanted a larger hall so that it could cut down on the number of concerts it gave. Today, attitudes

Model of the Major Hall showing Utzon's design for the ceiling constructed of plywood beams that spanned the depth of the hall and the stage machinery which was installed and later removed.

have changed and orchestras tend to prefer more concerts in better conditions than vice versa.

An interesting insight into Nutsch's situation came from the Irish architect Raymond McGrath who was working with Cremer in Berlin. In a letter sent to Ove Arup in April 1966, he related how Cremer 'told me that his assistant [Nutsch] had been in Sydney for two months without seeing Utzon. He was puzzled and considered recalling him. The impression I got was that he had been left 'holding the acoustic baby' and that he disliked this situation which he thought might reflect no credit on him. He had told me before that architects had a habit of bringing complete designs to him and expecting him to work miracles.' According to Wheatland, however, with whom Nutsch worked very closely, Nutsch himself never complained about the lack of meetings with Utzon.

The ceilings, too, were unresolved. Before Davis Hughes would agree to the A£60,000 needed for the mock-up of the ceiling beams to be made by Symonds, he asked for a structural report from Arups. The engineers had carried out intermittent design work on the auditoria ceilings between April

1964 and February 1965 based on Utzon's proposals of huge 50ft (15m)-long plywood beams spanning from the proscenium to the back of the hall. Work had ceased because Arups were unable to find out from the acoustics consultants what the ceiling would weigh. Arups thought the huge elements unnecessarily difficult to transport and almost impossible to erect without damage. They preferred their own suggestion, which used a steel framework to support smaller sections of ply that could be joined together on site. The Arups design was lighter, easier to erect, quicker, cheaper and would look exactly the same. But Utzon wanted the all-ply structure, which he felt was a more elegant and honest solution. He feared that the scarfed joints would leak acoustically and did not like the idea that the steel structure would be visible in the space between the ply ceiling and the concrete shell.

When Arups received the letter from the Government asking for a report, the engineers showed it to Utzon together with a draft reply to the Minister.

Utzon suggested that Arups should tell the PWD that they had submitted the report to him and that he would comment on the matter – he did not want Arups dealing direct with the department and asked for the draft comments to be resubmitted to him as a proper report. He was upset that the PWD had asked Arups directly for the information and saw this as an example of the engineers going behind his back to the client. He wrote angrily to Arups in London, with the formal 'Dear Sirs' greeting: 'I would therefore ask you to refer all future questions concerning Stage 3 which you might receive from the Minister for Public Works or from any other source direct to me and inform the parties who question you that they should apply for information from me.'

Following a meeting with Davis Hughes on 19 November 1965, when the Minister first became aware officially of the disagreement between the architect and the engineers over the design of the ceilings, Arups were asked to prepare a report on the structure as a part of a fuller report on the ceilings to be made by the architect.

Lewis was planning a trip to London over Christmas and the architects were keen to have the report prior to his departure. Wheatland suggested it did not have to be a very detailed report and insisted he received it before Lewis left for overseas. However, Arups did not want to limit their report to looking at the Utzon proposals alone, they wanted to compare them to their own solution and this would take longer to do.

Lewis's departure to London was a sensitive issue anyway in the Utzon office, as they believed that he was going to discuss with Zunz whether Arups should threaten to leave the job and give the Minister an ultimatum that they would only stay if the Government got rid of Utzon. They were correct in their suspicions regarding the former, but wrong on the latter. On 24 November, Lewis wrote to Zunz:

'We have virtually had no contact with Utzon or his staff over the past six months and we can recollect only eight meetings or [discussions] with them...'

'We have received no drawings from him or any requests for information and in fact, we are virtually doing nothing on Stage 3 except the design of the balconies of the major hall...'

'I saw quite unofficially, and definitely not to be repeated, a copy of the Minutes of the meeting he had on the 19th November... Utzon made a specific mention of having consulted Mr Miller [of Miller, Milston and Ferris], a consulting engineer for Symonds, about certain structural problems.... Since I haven't been told officially there is really nothing I can do about it but I do know that he is going out of his way to discredit us at every opportunity. I don't think the Government will consider any other consulting engineer but Utzon's statements and attitude are doing us irreparable harm in Sydney.

'It is a pity that the Government is using my trip as a deadline for forcing the pace. It possibly makes me look more the villain of the piece than is justified.'

Ove Arup drafted a reply:

'Your various letters about our relationship with Utzon have been very sad reading, and I think it seems now that we have come to the end of the road. It seems to me essential that we inform the client that we have lost the confidence of the Architect and that our collaboration therefore is extremely difficult and that we suggest to him that we should be released from further work on Stage 3 confining ourselves to the finalising of Stage 2.'

Zunz persuaded Arup not to send the letter and it remains to this day in Arups' London office files.

Meanwhile, Lewis believed Utzon was about to hand in his notice.

At a meeting of the architects and engineers with the Director of Public Works on 13 December 1965, it was agreed that the engineers' report should look at both proposals. During the meeting, Prip-Buus raised the subject of a report from Symonds' engineer, Peter Miller, which said that the Utzon proposals were workable. This annoyed Lewis, who suggested angrily that

Miller was not in a position to express opinions on the Opera House. Miller's report did not discuss the weight of the plywood beams or the ability of the shells to support them. This was a pretty fundamental issue – Arups feared that the beams as proposed could well bring the shells down.

While Lewis was away in London, the ceiling report was prepared by John Nutt. It stated that the maximum weight of the ceiling that could be suspended from the side shell arches was 60lbs/sq ft – the proposed schemes were all too heavy. The architect's scheme weighed 200lbs/sq ft at the front and 80lbs/sq ft at the rear, the suggested location of the hanger points were not feasible and the erection of units 50ft long and weighing 10 tons would be a problem. Nutt concluded that Arups much preferred the structural steel solution as being easier to erect, the weight could be supported by the existing structure, erection could take place before the building was waterproofed and the costs were considerably lower.

Utzon did not see the report until after 8 February 1966, when he returned from a six-week holiday to Japan and Hawaii.

On 10 February, Utzon sent the ceiling report to the Minister with a letter describing his disagreement with the engineers' findings. On the same day, he wrote two letters to Arups; one to Lewis saying that he could not accept the report, the other was to Ove Arup himself:

'The situation is very bad, not unlike the situation when the first scheme for the shells was about to be scrapped. I have a perfect and ingenious scheme which takes care of every aspect of the problems in building the ceilings of the hall. I want that to be built and it needs your support and your brilliant engineering because your partners here do not deal with the scheme and present an absolutely hopeless idea in a very amateurish way.

'I would also like to inform you that the behaviour of your partners here is not professional. They are dealing directly with my client behind my back in spite of my telling them not to do so. This leads us all into trouble.'

Before receiving this letter, Arup wrote to Utzon saying that he had heard he was thinking of resigning and advising him not to do so. But letters between London and Sydney were criss-crossing each other and developments were moving so fast that Arup's exhortations had little effect. While he was in Japan, Utzon had sent two postcards to Arup; on 13 February, Arup replied, by hand and in Danish, thanking him for the postcards and informing him that he had received the report on the ceilings from the Sydney office. Arup then goes on to outline what he saw as the key problem in the relationship between the two firms:

'As far as I can tell the report seems very sensible. It seems only natural to place the acoustic plates on a light iron construction. It nevertheless seems completely crazy to me that it is necessary to write such a report. If it is forwarded to the client it will clearly reveal the idiotic way we cooperate – or rather we do not cooperate. That can only do harm. But I understand that is the way you want it. First you will prepare a fully completed project, and then we are to state whether this is feasible from a constructional point of view. How far do you think we would have got if we had adopted this method for Stages 1 and 2? Is it not evident that we ought to submit a proposal to the client about which we both agree?'

He went on to say that he found Utzon's belief that Arups were working against him completely incomprehensible. He stressed that his whole team wanted to help him complete the building in the way that Utzon wanted, 'But we must of course make sure that this happens in a way which can be justified technically, that is our job, and that is also in your interest. If you do not believe this, well, then I really do not know what can be done. I hope that you will accept my outstretched hand.'

Arup then replied to Utzon's previous letter on 27 February:

'In your letter you appeal for my assistance. This pleases me, because I want nothing better than to help you and the job. But you do it in a most peculiar way, by insulting my trusted friends and collaborators. If you find Mick's [Lewis] and Nutt's scheme hopeless and amateurish, at least you could tell me what is wrong with it. I have not seen the drawings of our scheme except for the cross section shown in our report, but as far as I understand it, it gives exactly the same outward appearance as your scheme. But it weighs much less and can be built and costs less. So what is so frightfully wrong?

'You say that the situation is similar to that which occurred when we changed the shells to a ribbed construction without louvre walls. But that is not so. Then I disagreed with some of my people about the feasibility of building the scheme as you wanted it – with inside ribs and without louvre walls. I thought it could be done, and I also preferred this solution from an architectural point of view. So, in spite of the disruption it caused, I supported you against some of my own people. But this time there is no difference in the architecture, as far as I know, and I have absolute faith in Mick and Co. But of course I have not seen your complete scheme yet, so I keep an open mind.'

By the time Utzon received the letter he had already left the job.

Utzon did not like Lewis's report because it merely commented on schemes as presented; it did not attempt to refine the structure or to reduce the amount of plywood and to make it work as one might normally expect from the engineer.

Nutt was not the only one unhappy with the design of the plywood beams. Corbet Gore did not like the idea of trying to build them. 'They were massive plywood boxes,' he said, 'all of which had their finished surfaces, so they couldn't be damaged… They had to be joined together in the air, under the shells, which means you couldn't handle them by crane because the shells were blanketing out the crane hook. So they would have had to be manoeuvred in on some sort of trolley and then lifted up by rigging with very little space for your rigging between the edge of the beams and the shells.'

He did admit that they had overcome many equally complex construction problems on the Opera House in the past. 'If we had to we probably could have come up with a solution which, many dollars later, would have worked.' Utzon suggested it wasn't Gore's problem. The erection of the plywood would be subcontracted, he said.

Despite the differing views of the teams regarding the construction of the ceilings, Lewis felt that it was unwise for their disagreements to be publicly aired and on 18 February he wrote to the Minister to suggest that 'scrutiny by you should be deferred until we are able to reach complete agreement with the architect on the technical matters concerned.'

Utzon, however, was under the impression that Lewis had retracted the report, although the wording of Lewis's letter, is unequivocal. Whether the report had been 'deferred' or 'retracted' became a major issue during the debates surrounding Utzon's departure with the Minister being accused of dishonesty by referring to the Arups report when he knew it had been withdrawn.

Lewis's letter continued: 'Such agreement is the normally accepted practice in all work involving collaboration between Architect and Engineer, without which the client would be placed in the invidious position of having to choose between conflicting recommendations. …We feel sure that agreement can be reached soon.' Five days later, at a meeting in Arups' office between Lewis, Nutt, Wheatland and Prip-Buus, it was. The architects presented three alternative studies that lightened the structure by using the acoustic layers structurally. Acoustic insulation was provided by the top and bottom flanges of the beam, but a lot of the weight was in the vertical planes of the radii; by reducing the weight of these it seemed they had the problem solved. The minutes read:

'Mr Lewis's comment to these schemes was that he preferred alternative "C" and that he indicated without further study, he was sure that scheme would work structurally and lessened the weight problems inherent in the sketch scheme indicated on the Architect's drawing no. SOH 1380.'

Arups agreed to develop version 'C'.

Lewis wrote to London on 24 February saying, '...they have hurriedly drawn some alternative sections which to a large extent embody Nutt's plywood box section scheme but persist with large sections ...they have agreed to using open web girders towards the front of the auditorium where the weight is excessive – we have the beginnings of a workable scheme.'

The Minister's office drafted a reply to Lewis's letter of 18 February: 'I am pleased to note that you and the Architect will collaborate to reach complete agreement on the technical matters concerned. I will await the receipt of a joint recommendation when the difficulties have been solved. It is noted that this should be received in the near future.'

However, the letter was overtaken by events and remained, unsent, in the Ministry files.

CHAPTER 6
'YOU HAVE FORCED ME TO LEAVE'

With the difficulties of the auditoria ceilings all but solved, Utzon might have thought things were about to improve. However, the pressures continued to build up.

On 24 February 1966, there was a meeting between Stan Haviland and representatives of the ABC to discuss various fairly mundane matters, such as lighting, where to put TV vans during broadcasts and wiring. At the meeting, Warwick Mehaffey, ABC's acoustics engineer, dropped a bombshell. He announced that the Major Hall was quite unsuitable for concerts by the Sydney Symphony Orchestra because it did not have enough seats to make it financially viable, there was not enough volume to give the required reverberation time, the rehearsal room was not big enough, there was inadequate provision for television and recording cables and, to cap it all, the problem of harbour noises penetrating the auditoria seemed unsolved.

Mehaffey had plenty of experience in building concert halls; he had designed the acoustics for the ABC studios in Perth and, in 1966, was working on the acoustics for the Perth Concert Hall and the Adelaide Festival Theatre. He was greatly influenced by the work of the BBC Research Department in England, one of the leading centres of acoustical research at the time and which took a somewhat traditional view of the design of space for music. Tom Somerville, head of the department, wrote to Mehaffey after Utzon's resignation: 'I am very interested in your remarks about the Sydney Opera House. Many years ago I was asked by one of the entrants in the competition if I would be prepared to help him with the acoustics, but when he explained the specification, which was that it should be suitable for opera of all types and also symphonic music, I refused to consider it.' Somerville's and Mehaffey's positions were to be crucial in the decisions on the Major Hall that would be taken post-Utzon.

Haviland left the meeting visibly shocked. Mehaffey's comments soon got back to Talbot Duckmanton, the ABC's general manager, who was having a lunch meeting with Premier Askin the next day. Duckmanton's comments on the ABC's position on the Major Hall over lunch would surely have affected Askin's response to the developments of the next few days.

Utzon can hardly be blamed for not being fully aware of the ABC's requirements – even at the meeting of SOHEC on 17 February 1966 it is noted that, 'a reply is awaited from the ABC as to their possible future use of the halls and ancillary accommodation,' but it added to the pressures on him at a difficult time.

Utzon was also facing serious financial problems. He had recently received a substantial tax bill from the Australian authorities, despite the fact that he had already paid tax in Denmark. According to Drew, he told his secretary that he would either have to reach a settlement with the Government or leave the country. On top of this, the 'cheque book' control first suggested by Wood to Ryan was having its effect.

Until the latter part of 1965, Utzon had been receiving regular sums of money from SOHEC to cover salaries and operating expenses. These amounts were advances to be reconciled with his fees at the end of the job. In order to put some pressure on Utzon to produce drawings, Davis Hughes followed Wood's advice and fees would only be paid on the basis of work done. In October 1965, Utzon told his staff he may have to close down the office because his cash position was so bad, and on 15 October he wrote to Haviland: 'I am sure you understand when I talked to you that my office would have to close down if I do not get the fee immediately, as I have no resources. Will you please help me get A£24,000 before the 25th September [he presumably meant October]?' His plea did the trick and he was paid the A£24,000 in November and a further A£20,000 in December.

He also then made a claim for A£51,626 (A$102,000 – the Australian monetary system went decimal on 14 February 1966) fees for work carried out in his office on the stage machinery five years earlier. James Thomas remembers spending much of his time in Hellebæk in 1960 trying to fit the stage machinery under the roofs. It was clearly work that Utzon had carried out, but should he be paid for it? He had already been paid architect's fees for work on the stage layout, but now viewed the work on machinery as engineering and thus eligible for additional fees. His claim would seem to conflict with his views in 1962. On 8 November of that year, he sent a letter to Zunz about fees to be forwarded to the client, which said that, following the resignation of Messrs Balslev and Partners, the stage technique would be controlled by Professor Unruh's and Utzon's office. He suggested that this would actually save 3.5 per cent on the fees, 'because the architect has done a great part of the work in his office'. There was no mention of additional fees at that time.

Utzon claimed the money in October 1965 in the hope of improving his dire financial position. In November, Ron Gilling and Jack Farrington, immediate past president representing the RAIA, were asked to advise the PWD. According to the notes of the meeting, Farrington did not believe that Utzon was entitled to fees. 'What the Architect does in his own office is part of his function as the Architect for which his architectural fee suffices.' In any case there was no prior consent of the client to the arrangement. Gilling concurred, but with the reservation that he would like to see the documents relating to the architect's appointment.

Utzon wrote to Davis Hughes on 10 February 1966 repeating his claim for fees. On 15 February the Minister replied, saying 'This matter has been carefully investigated and I am advised that there is no record of an agreement appointing you as your own specialist consultant for this work, in addition to your work as Architect ...before a final decision is made it is essential to know what other payments you are seeking in respect of this work.' The PWD had been looking into the claim but did not report until 3 March, when it recommended a payment of A£31,319; however, the Government Architect, Ted Farmer, was not convinced and suggested the matter be referred to the RAIA for assessment.

On the fateful morning of Monday 28 February 1966, Utzon, accompanied by Wheatland, went to see Davis Hughes to discuss the fees. The Minister informed Utzon that he was willing to agree to fee payments of A$20,000 per month as advances on fees, subject to the recommendation of the liaison architect after inspection of progress.

Utzon then raised the issue of the fees for the work on the stage machinery. Davis Hughes promised him a decision 'this week'. Utzon responded, 'You are always putting me off.' The Minister repeated his promise, at which point Utzon said he would resign. Davis Hughes replied that Utzon 'could not keep on saying this' and that it was 'no way to address a Minister of the Crown'. Utzon then walked out of the meeting followed by Wheatland.

Haviland was out of town so Davis Hughes called in Ashworth of the SOHEC who arrived at the Minister's office at 2.30pm. While they were discussing what Utzon's intentions might be, a letter arrived from the architect. It raised the issue of the stage machinery fees and a lack of collaboration by the PWD.

'I have been forced to set the 15th February, 1966 as the final date for the receipt of this payment, and as you could not, at this late date, 28th February, satisfy me on this, you have forced me to leave the job.

'As I explained to you, and as you also know from meetings and discussions, there has been no collaboration on the most vital items of the job in the last months from your Department's side, and this also forces me to leave the job as I see clearly that you do not respect me as an architect.

'I have therefore today given my staff notice of dismissal.'

'I will notify the Consultants and Contractors and I will have cleared the office of my belongings and you will receive my final account before March 14, 1966.'

Although Utzon later claimed that this did not mean 'I have resigned', it was accepted by many who read it as such. However, on 8 March, Utzon wrote to Davis Hughes: 'I did not resign as Architect of the Sydney Opera House. I stated that in view of the fact that payments due to me were being withheld and that my Client has withheld the decision and collaboration which are normally the duty of any client, I will be forced to leave the job.'

According to Bill Wheatland, 'Utzon had no intention of resigning when he wrote the letter, he was "stressed beyond imagination" and wrote to the Minister "straight from the heart" in hindsight not a wise thing to do'. Wheatland suggested the letter be vetted by a solicitor but Utzon refused.

Utzon seemed convinced that Davis Hughes would have to call him back, and asked his staff not to seek other work in that eventuality. He believed strongly that no one else could complete the building and that when he was called back he would be in a stronger position.

Davis Hughes then called in Corbet Gore and Lewis. Lewis recalls: 'The Minister said that "I have received a letter of resignation from the Architect and I have discussed it with my colleagues and we are going to accept the resignation. We would like to know what you think we should do." And I said "I think you should finish the construction because it is well under way, and treat it like a found object and put it out to a design competition to decide what to put into that space." He [Davis Hughes] said he couldn't do that and had to get on with the job, that was what he was commissioned to do.'

The Minister then asked what Arups' reaction was likely to be. Lewis said he still had to consult his colleagues, but he could see no reason why the firm should resign. During the evening the press contacted the Minister, having heard that Utzon had dismissed his staff; they were given copies of the "resignation" letter. In London, Ove Arup spent the day trying unsuccessfully to contact Utzon by telephone.

The next day, Davis Hughes sent a confidential minute to the Cabinet setting out the position with Utzon. On the stage machinery fees, he suggested, 'the Architect's entitlement is not clear.' But he said he had promised a decision this week. On the subject of lack of collaboration, he commented that, 'it is in this area that the real cause for the Architect's action lies.' The Minister then cited the construction of the 'plywood theatres' (presumably the ceilings); the employment of Ralph Symonds Ltd for work to the value of A$2million on the ceilings and glass walls, and the construction of plywood prototypes at a cost of A$120,000 as outstanding issues.

Presumably referring to his discussions with Ron Gilling, Davis Hughes added: 'Anticipating that this position may arise I have discussed the method whereby the Opera House could be completed with the Government Architect and Senior Officers of the NSW Chapter of the Institute. I am satisfied that a means can be found to complete the planning and supervision of the work ...I have already taken steps to ensure that progress on Stage 2 will not be interrupted.'

Wood's report in August 1965 had set out a plan illustrating how Utzon's team could be reinforced by other architectural skills; it is clear the PWD had been giving much thought to increasing Utzon's productivity and that such measures might bring about his resignation. By Tuesday 1 March 1966, the PWD had prepared a paper illustrating a 'Basis of Proposal' whereby Utzon would work as design consultant to a firm or consortium of private architects, working under the Government Architect for detailed planning, execution and supervision of the work. Alternatively, the Department suggested, Utzon 'accepts without reservation that the Minister is Principal and that normal relationship of Architect and client exists. The Architect to meet the Client's reasonable requirements.'

The final denouement came as no surprise to the PWD; Farmer, the Government Architect, had been told by R A Johnson some time prior to

Utzon's departure that it was likely he would be called in to sort out the problems at Bennelong Point. Davis Hughes' comment also suggests that he viewed the discussions he had had with the RAIA in a more substantive light than Gilling did.

His comments regarding progress of Stage 2 probably refer to a meeting he had with representatives from the major consultants – Arups, Steensen and Varming, Julius Poole & Gibson, Rider Hunt and Partners and the contractor Hornibrook. The notes by the Director of Public Works minute that the Minister 'looked to them for their future co-operation in the project and this was assured by them'.

A handwritten note at the bottom of the minute sums up the position in which the protagonists jointly found themselves.

'Lewis, Noe (Hornibrook) and Jones were critical of the present situation and doubted Utzon's ability to administer Stage 3.

'Policy of experimentation: no organisation: no co-ordination of consultants: no control: grave disquiet of those who would have to work under him: no working drawings to action, to advise on, to plan on or to estimate on: continual change. No appreciation of cost: no appreciation of design, etc. before prototype.'

Not only had Utzon lost the confidence of his client. He had also lost the confidence of his consultants.

The Minister announced Utzon's 'resignation' in Parliament on the afternoon of Tuesday 1 March 1966.

At 5.00pm that day, Utzon, accompanied by Wheatland and Prip-Buus, met with the Minister at Ashworth's request. Neither party was in a conciliatory mood. Utzon brought with him a list of nine demands phrased as though he was negotiating from a position of strength, and included:

'Architect requires a statement from the Minister that the Architect will give final approval for all details of the Opera House.

'The Architect requires a statement from the Minister to the consultants that the Architect is in charge and that the client will not go directly to the consultants or to the contractor.

'The mock-up proposal for plywood structures which was delivered to the Minister be accepted immediately.'

The meeting continued for two and a half hours and ended without agreement on a single point. The Minister later suggested to Ashworth that the spirit in which the nine points had been prepared indicated an attitude

Protesters gather outside the Opera House site in support of Utzon's reinstatement.

that did not 'promise prospects for reconciliation'.

At 8.00pm, Davis Hughes met with Farmer and Gilling. The Minister opened the meeting with the question, 'My Architect has resigned. What do I do?'

'Get him back,' replied Gilling.

From the Minister's comments, Gilling got the impression that, if Utzon came back at all, the Government Architect would be in charge and not Utzon. The Minister asked Gilling's advice on how architectural services could be provided to finish the project.

'I told him that a consortium of architectural firms was quite impractical and inadvisable – and furthermore it was not the function of the Institute to provide names of architects in circumstances such as this. I advised him that I would give him all the assistance I could to achieve a reconciliation with Utzon, but I would never give him names.'

On Wednesday 2 March Gilling held a meeting of the Council of the NSW Chapter and was pressed to make immediate statements demanding that Utzon be reinstated; he found some difficulty in convincing members that Utzon had not been fired. Already a division was growing among members of the RAIA, between those who believed Utzon should be reinstated as sole architect in charge and those who were willing to accept a compromise as the only way of convincing the Government to have him back at all.

Gilling went to Utzon's office where he offered the support of the RAIA and confirmed the offer in writing. He never received an answer.

A deputation of some 30 architects, led by Harry Seidler, then met with Gilling to get his assurance that the Council would support Utzon and that there was no consortium or panel of architects to complete the work. They were given assurances on both counts. Seidler was then invited to join an RAIA select committee meeting that was about to start.

Reports of this meeting differ. Seidler's understanding of what went on clearly spurred him to action in the campaign to bring Utzon back. Gilling's version of the meeting is that the select committee did not discuss any solution that was based on the premise that Utzon would not continue on the project. 'We refused to accept that reconciliation was not possible – this was our only objective. Several methods of assisting Jørn Utzon were explored – it was agreed that he should be offered or provided with technical assistance with regard to tendering procedures. By way of example we discussed the names of architects as being the type of people who could give Utzon assistance.'

Seidler felt the events to be of such import that he signed a 'Statutory Declaration' on 28 March which quoted Gilling as saying, 'The Minister of Public Works wants our help to suggest a panel of architects to complete the Opera House. We must give him this. What I envisage is a man with Utzon's spirit of design – Mr B Mortlock, someone to do the working drawings – Mr O Jarvis, because he had worked on the Opera House plans in Denmark some years ago, and a firm to do the general administration – Edwards, Madigan & Torzillo, because they get along well with the Government architects.'

Gilling did not become aware of the existence of the declaration until years later in 2003. 'I wish I had known of this at the time' he stated after reading the document. 'Nothing was ever said which could remotely resemble what Seidler alleged ...If I had known of the Stat Dec I could have produced one from each member present to refute such an allegation.'

Such discrepancies of recall reflect the gulf that separated the two parties. Whatever the truth regarding the meeting, Seidler wanted Utzon reinstated on his own terms, the Institute was prepared to support the idea of an architectural team to provide Utzon with the necessary back up.

The next day, Seidler took part in a protest meeting of several hundred architects and students bearing 'Bring Back Utzon', 'Utzon in Charge' and, more humorously, 'Consortium Abortium' placards, outside the gates of the Opera House site. Following the protest, a petition of 3,000 signatures was delivered to Parliament House and Seidler went to meet the Premier. Gilling took a dim view of this turn of events and felt that it was dividing the profession. 'This fragmented approach did much to damage Utzon and did nothing to influence Government officialdom.'

On 4 March, Gilling wrote to Davis Hughes setting out the RAIA's position. He described some of the critical factors of the contract, such as the premature start on site, and that prototypes are necessary and winners of competitions should be commissioned to carry out the whole work.

The letter also criticized the separate contracts between the client and Utzon and between the client and Arups:

'It is a fundamental principle in any building project that the architect should be the co-ordinator of the work of the various consultants employed for design and construction and the Chapter believes that much of the trouble which exists at the Sydney Opera House arises because of this system of separate control by consultants and this has been detrimental to the satisfactory design and construction of the project.'

The letter stated that the NSW Chapter recommended that Utzon should remain in full design control with some provisions put in place for proper administrative and technical control.

In a press release, the RAIA stated: 'The New South Wales Chapter is of the opinion that the true spirit of this project cannot be achieved unless Mr Utzon continues as the designing architect.' This drew criticism from the pro-Utzon lobby who felt it implied that the RAIA had accepted Utzon's resignation 'at face value'. And there were rumours that the Institute had been collaborating with Davis Hughes and a panel had been formed to take over the project. A statement denying that this was the case was issued by Gilling; this was greeted with great relief in the Utzon office where there had been suspicions that the RAIA would follow the Government line.

However, their relief was short lived. On Monday 7 March, Utzon met again with the Minister who presented him with the 'Basis for Proposal'. This set out the points of a 'new relationship' and proposed that Utzon would be appointed as 'Design Architect' with full responsibility for originating and supervising development of design. He was to collaborate with a team headed by the Government Architect who would be responsible for the planning of the design and construction programme, production of plans and specifications, tenders, consultants, contractors and costs.

Utzon responded with his own modified proposal which suggested that, 'Mr Utzon is to be confirmed as the architect in control of the building fully in accordance with the contract between him and the Sydney Opera House Executive Committee.' He also stated that the architect's office should act as the executive and administrative organization responsible to the Minister for planning and construction. It was a straight rebuttal of Davis Hughes' proposal. This was a curious reaction from Utzon because the Minister's proposal was not unlike the one he had recently accepted for the Schauspielhaus in Zurich.

Utzon was backed in his stand by the 'Utzon in Charge' group who would settle for nothing less than full reinstatement. However, Gilling was of the view that the Basis provided room for manoeuvre and convinced Davis Hughes to meet Utzon again saying that, in his view, Utzon was being badly advised by his supporters. The only concession Gilling obtained was that Davis Hughes would agree to meet if Utzon requested the meeting.

Gilling told the Minister that he should make public the reasons why he would not re-engage Utzon. Davis Hughes declined saying, 'I will not be party to ruining that man's reputation.'

Certainly the NSW Parliamentary debates held on 2 March and 9 March concerning the Opera House shed little light on the situation and were focused largely on the matter of cost with accusations and counter-accusations of each party's inability to control the contract.

On 9 March, Gilling wrote to Utzon to tell him that the Chapter Council had agreed that the Basis of Proposal should be very seriously considered as a starting point for negotiations. In the letter, Gilling pleads with him not to close the door and talks about a 'partnership' arrangement instead of the more inflammatory 'Design Architect' role.

Utzon agreed to meet Davis Hughes again, and since the Minister had insisted there should be no publicity it was suggested by Gilling that the meeting should be held at a motel, in which he owned shares, in Lane Cove on the evening of 10 March.

On the morning of that day, Gilling released a press statement which said:

'The Institute believes in the competency of Mr Utzon as an architect but supports moves to provide proper administration and technical control of the construction. It is obvious that the architectural profession deplores any situation where costs appear to be rising uncontrolled and construction time is unlimited. For anyone to say that Mr Utzon is entirely to blame for the present situation is ridiculous.'

Early on in the Lane Cove meeting, Davis Hughes drew an organization chart which, according to the meeting notes shows 'Utzon as a full member of the panel on the design side'. In actual fact, it shows Utzon out on a limb. It was unlikely to impress Utzon, and even less the 'Utzon in Charge' group. The Government Architect was at the top of the chart, responsible for the consultants and the Architects' Panel which consisted of 'Construction', 'Staff' and 'Design'. The last – literally squeezed onto the edge of the paper in the Minister's sketch – was to be Utzon's role. Davis Hughes proffered, '... there is room for compromise within that proposal of mine.' The general tone of the meeting was conciliatory. Farmer sympathized with Utzon about the lack of a proper brief for the building. Utzon asked for money:

Utzon: I require A£5000 [A$10,000] tomorrow to pay the staff.
Humphrey (Director PWD): We will pay it tomorrow.

Davis Hughes: The payment is approved.

Utzon was concerned that he would be entering a partnership with people he did not know. 'You will not put my enemies there such as Bunning…', he said at one point. The Minister was keen that Utzon should come to a decision about the proposed organization within four days, prior to the next Cabinet meeting. Utzon said he needed 14 days to consult his office and his consultants.

Farmer believed that Utzon had very nearly agreed to the proposal, but was concerned that the 'Utzon in Charge' campaigners might get him to change his mind.

The summary at the end of the PWD's notes says:

'I think it is fair to say, and this could be the basis of a press statement, that he has accepted the conditions provided he is given time to condition his mind thereto and make such checks as he needs to verify that from his point of view it is workable. Whilst he is doing this, it is most important that we keep in close contact with him to continue to maintain our position. He must not be allowed to isolate himself from our thinking and more importantly to be influenced by others to the contra view.'

The same day, Zunz sent a confidential telegram to Utzon which read:

'I know that it is very late for me to plead with you. I don't care how difficult your or anyone else's position, but possibility of Opera House without you too bleak to contemplate. Over many years you have not spared yourself nor have you spared others who you have stimulated with your conception and you cannot ditch them at this stage. Even if you have to make what appears to you to be a bad compromise please at least give it a try. Your undoubted persuasive powers will then safeguard the design which after all is the main thing. For the sake of the job, family, friends, admirers and not least the people of Sydney please help the government find a solution even if it means turning the other cheek.'

Zunz did not receive a reply. It was being suggested that Arups should resign in solidarity with Utzon. Arup wanted to walk away from the job in what Zunz describes as a 'visceral urge'. However, Zunz persuaded him that there was no real reason for the firm to resign since they had a separate contract. 'There was no way we could walk away from a contract where the client had treated us so well.' Lewis, closer to the coal-face, did not think that resigning should be contemplated.

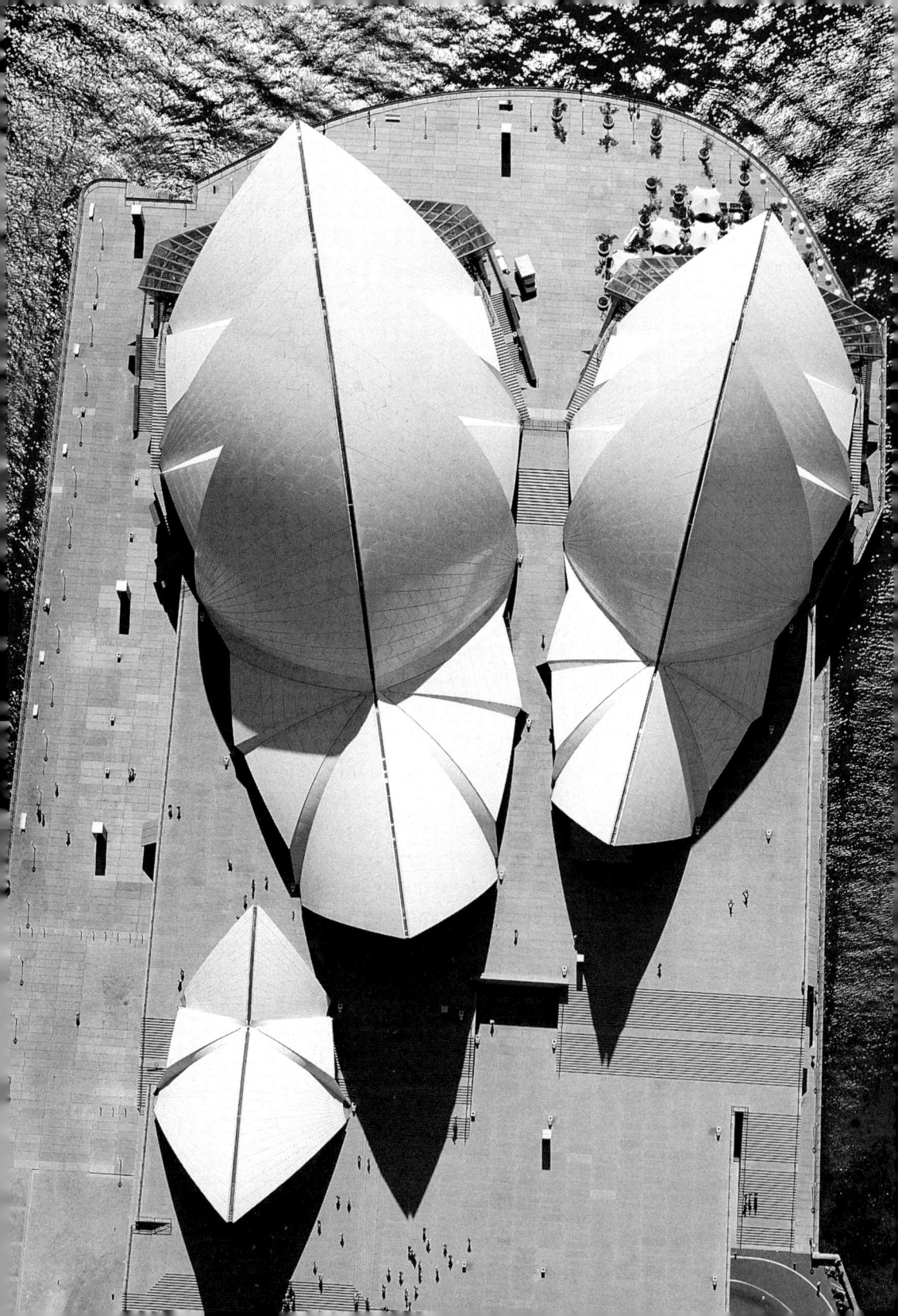

Had Arups decided to resign, the impact would have been huge. Certainly, Davis Hughes believed that he would have had little option but to resign himself in such an eventuality. This in turn could have led to a vote of no confidence and since the Liberal/Country Party Coalition enjoyed only a slim majority, the result could have gone either way.

A cheque for A$10,000 duly arrived on 11 March from the PWD together with a letter insisting that Utzon reply to the Minister's proposals by 10.00am on Tuesday 15 March.

Also on 11 March, the ABC general manager, Duckmanton, called on the Director of Public Works and reiterated the points made by Mehaffey a fortnight before. The Director informed him that, '…the Department would necessarily be becoming more involved in this project with a heavier responsibility for planning and building, according to requirements of the future users.'

On 14 March, a meeting was held at Sydney Town Hall to call for the reinstatement of Utzon. Around 1,200 people attended, about half of them students. Seidler told the audience that the purpose of the meeting was to avert a cultural tragedy and to prevent a travesty of justice. He claimed that the campaign against the architect was premeditated and planned with the help of publicity experts to bring about certain political aims. He criticized the Government's organization of the project and blamed the liaison architect, Wood, who, he said, was not in sympathy with the project. He criticized Arups for being unreasonable and the arrangement whereby they were directly responsible to the client.

He said it was impossible for Utzon to come back as a 'sort of designer' with an 'insignificant position on the team'.

'This building cannot be dealt with as one would build a factory. If Mr Utzon leaves, a crime will have been committed against future generations of Australians and if this should happen world history will never forgive us.'

Seidler had roused opinion around the world in support of Utzon and received letters from a number of leading names, including Louis Kahn, Felix Candela, Richard Neutra, Kenzo Tange, Aldo Van Eyck and Ralph Erskine. In the light of the atmosphere surrounding the resignation, and the lack of clear information surrounding Utzon's departure, it is understandable that the international architectural community should have been so supportive. However, some years later Kenzo Tange told Zunz that, in similar circumstances, he himself would never have resigned.

Utzon replied to the Minister as requested. His letter, dated 15 March 1966, rejected the proposed organization.

'It would seem that I am merely to prepare designs in accordance with instructions and leave it to others to supervise construction. Such a proposal is not only unpractical but quite unacceptable to me.

'I am at all times prepared to work with them [a team of leading architects] as your representatives, but not under them.'

He added an appendix to the letter, which was to prove prophetic. 'It is not I but the Sydney Opera House that creates all the enormous difficulties.' He said that the new team of architects would start from zero. 'They will be coming to you as soon as they realize the difficulties.'

Lewis wrote to Arup and Zunz on 18 March:

'It seems now that the break between Utzon and the Government is beyond repair and Davis Hughes has closed the door to further negotiations. I have the feeling that Utzon wanted to accept their terms but was too proud to say it directly.... A contributory factor to his attitude has been the advice he has been taking – the marches, mass meetings and misinformed emotional statements by all and sundry, have tended to boost his ego at a time when a grain of humility might have solved the entire situation. In spite of my previous distrust and misgivings concerning Utzon, I feel terribly sad for his sake at having to give up this project after so many years.'

Lewis reported that he was concerned about the statement by the RAIA that criticized the manner in which separate contracts were entered into between the client and the architect and the structural engineers for Stage 1. '...the Chapter believes that much of the trouble which exists at the Sydney Opera House arises because of this system of separate control by consultants and this has been detrimental to the satisfactory design and construction of the project.'

Lewis arranged to meet Gilling to discuss the statement, but when he arrived at the Chapter offices Gilling had been called away to a meeting with Davis Hughes. Lewis was mollified by a member of the Chapter Executive Committee, Geoff Moline, who said that the statement was intended as a criticism of the Government's handling of the contract and not a criticism of Arups. 'Towards the end of the meeting,' Lewis wrote, 'Gilling turned up in an extremely distraught state having just been told by the Minister that further negotiations would be impossible.'

With work on Stage 3 grinding to a halt, the staff at Arups, apart from those on site, had little to do. To give them some work, Lewis had been discussing the preparation of as-built drawings of the work to date with Farmer. During the discussion the Government Architect expanded on his ideas on the choice of architects to replace Utzon. Farmer's intention at that stage was not a panel of architects but to co-opt two architectural firms by employing a partner from each – one to act as design architect and one to act as coordinating architect. At the time, Lewis was under the impression that Farmer was going to choose Ken Woolley of Anchor Mortlock Murray and Woolley, who had previously worked in the PWD and designed the State Office Block on Macquarie Street – generally considered one of the best new buildings in Sydney of the time. 'If I am right in my surmise then there is a good chance that the design architect will be of a very high calibre.' Lewis's surmise was correct, but Woolley did not want the job. He was not keen on the idea of completing someone else's work and he was at the beginning of his career with a lot of projects and a large staff; the all-consuming nature of the Opera House would have created problems with his existing clients.

On 28 March, a special general meeting of the NSW Chapter of the RAIA passed a vote of confidence in the actions of the President and the Council. The vote was 369 votes in favour and 283 against. The meeting was run strictly by the Institute's by-laws and students were not permitted to vote. Had they done so the outcome would have been different, and the decision to stick by the rules caused much ill feeling among Utzon's supporters. The motion accentuated the divisions between the RAIA and the 'Utzon in Charge' campaign – while everyone who spoke supported it, the methods of approaching the reinstatement of Utzon differed.

The pressure was taking its toll on Utzon. Late one night, Lis Utzon telephoned Gilling at his office and pleaded, '…please do not try to keep Jørn here, he is not a well man.' However, Gilling did not let this conversation deter him in his quest to broker a reconciliation with Davis Hughes to retain the services of Utzon as the architect of the Opera House.

Gilling had one further meeting with the Minister on 18 April in a last-ditch attempt to bring the two together. Gilling went to the meeting with the full knowledge of Peter Kollar, the chairman of the 'Utzon in Charge' group, and believed that when Kollar said that Utzon was prepared to negotiate, he had Utzon's approval for such a statement. However, Utzon sent a letter to the Secretary of the NSW Chapter, dated 18 April but not received until the next day, saying that he would only return on the basis of his last offer. He accused the RAIA of not 'supporting the rights of an architect', and confusing the client as to the responsibilities of an architect.

The next morning, the papers reported that the names of a panel of architects would be announced later the following day.

Peter Hall rang Gilling during the day to inform him of his place on the panel; it became clear to Gilling that Hall was a reluctant recruit and would step down if Utzon were to offer to return. Hall rang Utzon but was told by him that he would only go back when asked, after the new architects had failed. He added that, when he came back, he would remove everything that the new architects had done.

The panel was duly announced. Peter Hall was to be the design architect. As an ex-member of the PWD, his qualities were known to Farmer and his assistant, Charlie Weatherburn, who put the list together. Hall had grown up in the PWD office. He had been a trainee in a system that produced high flyers like Ken Woolley and Peter Webber (later to become Government Architect). According to Farmer 'Hall was a very fine designer and a man of parts with an arts, as well as architecture degree... so I asked him if he could do it. He was in a terrible state over it. He knew what he was letting himself in for'. David Littlemore of Rudder, Littlemore and Rudder was to supervise the construction. Lionel Todd of Hanson Todd and Partners was invited to oversee the contract documentation on the recommendation of Davis Hughes. Farmer did not like this, he did not get on well with Todd and there were frequent arguments in the ensuing years. The arrangement divided the various skills required within the design and construction processes in a similar way to that which Davis Hughes had proposed at the Lane Cove motel meeting under the heading of 'Architects' Panel'. Farmer himself made up the fourth member of the team.

Gilling wrote to Davis Hughes one last time on the matter, telling the Minister that:

'...our position is made extremely difficult by your reluctance to state publicly why Mr Utzon could not be re-employed as sole architect. I understand your desire to protect my profession and its members from criticism over the handling of the Opera House project but I can assure you that far greater damage to our professional reputation is being done by not making the reasons known.'

Lewis thought it was time there was a statement made by somebody 'in the know' on the situation, and that Arups were in a position to do this.

However, he disagreed with Ove Arup's desire to support the full reinstatement of the architect. He wrote to Arup on 15 April:

'Utzon has failed to perform his function as the Architect for this project, even though his reputation as a leader in the architectural world has been almost entirely based on this one project. This anomaly must be explained and in order to do this it is necessary to outline in full the role we have played in bringing this scheme to its present state – also, by extending this argument, it is easy to see that a similar collaboration with a responsible architect looking after the preparation of working drawings, administration and control of construction in Stage 3 would not only be workable but would probably be the only basis on which the project could be completed with Utzon remaining the designer. This is what the Government have offered him and we should support it.'

He concluded the letter with a perceptive comment regarding the new team of architects. 'They may find that there are serious gaps in the proposals set out by Utzon which will lead to compromises and subsequent criticism that the scheme has been ruined by their efforts.'

Zunz and Arup arrived in Sydney on 24 April and immediately attempted to meet Utzon, but he refused to see them.

Four days later, Utzon flew out of Sydney and wrote to Arup from Hawaii. His letter revealed all the bitter resentments that had built up against the engineers over the past year. It is hard to believe that the relationship between the two which, five years earlier, had been so warm and so productive, could have reached such a nadir.

'You have shown an incredible lack of understanding of what an architect and the work of an architect is, not only in your personal letter to Lis and myself, but also and more seriously through your own and your firm's behaviour in the case of the Sydney Opera House and through your statement to the client as well as the press.

'You have thoroughly revealed your unlimited over-estimation of your own – the engineer's – part in this case, an over-estimation which causes your deliberate destruction of my – the architect's – position and possibilities to finalize the building. I need point out only three of many examples:

'Your firm's completely misleading report of the shell construction which you sent to the client behind my back…

'Your own destructive conversation with the previous client, Minister for Public Works, Mr Ryan, in London, a conversation in which you demanded a new contract according to which I was supposed to be a designer only subordinate to the engineer.

'Your memorandum to M.L. [Michael Lewis] when he started.'

'As you have not acted on my last letter and requested that the client take me back as architect fully in charge, making this your condition for continuing your job as structural engineer, you have proved that you still do not want to understand that the Sydney Opera House will be destroyed completely if I am not fully in charge and that you do not want to respect the opinion of many of the world's foremost architects, who as you know have supported me 100 per cent.'

In May 1966, the Danish daily publication, *Politiken*, placed Utzon's criticisms in the public realm: 'Arup has not taken part in the construction for the last three years. His Sydney branch did it and they worked very independently.' Utzon told them. 'Arup's fault is that he also has ambitions as an architect. He wanted to interfere with the architectural shaping and he dominated the whole construction. ...Later he said all I had to do was to hang my architecture on his construction.'

Arup responded by saying that it was never his ambition to be the architect. 'These are new statements from Utzon but I understand that lately a change in his attitude had taken place. I wish Utzon would return to Sydney. Statements like this don't help him.'

Zunz refutes any suggestion that Arups asked Ryan for a new contract where Utzon was subordinate: 'It is simply not true.'

Also in *Politiken*, Steen Eiler Rasmussen, the renowned Danish architect and town planner and Utzon's former teacher, continued the attacks upon Arup. He wrote suggesting that it was unfortunate that Utzon did not have someone like Arup by his side to support him and inferred that Arup himself was too old at over 70 and, anyway, had withdrawn from the work in Sydney some time previously. In reply, Arup wrote to Eiler Rasmussen protesting: 'Had he accepted my help none of this would have happened ...It is Jørn who has withdrawn his co-operation from me.'

But before he received this letter, Eiler Rasmussen had already written to Arup seeking his help as 'the only person in the world who at this moment may be able to bring common sense to the affair of the Sydney Opera House.' He described how he had spent a couple of months in Sydney the year before and, from what he had seen during that time, the break came as no surprise to him because of the Government-orchestrated vendetta against the architect. 'He was subjected to daily attacks by the press, in part for the excessive cost, in part for the excessive time the work took and in part for his fees. Every day whilst I was in Sydney there were attacks on him in one way or other, as if he was a foreign swindler, who had come to extract money from the poor government.'

Eiler Rasmussen took the view that Arup's criticism of the auditoria ceilings had given the Minister the excuse to get rid of Utzon and that the firm should take the blame for the whole fiasco.

Arup, on the other hand, blamed Utzon's state of mind. He replied to Eiler Rasmussen:

'What motivates him, what causes his strange behaviour, here I can only guess. But I am convinced that this is not a conflict between Utzon and the Government or Utzon and O A & Partners, it is a conflict within Utzon himself. And the only hope of saving Utzon's dream is if a friend or friends of his whom he trusts – and I do not belong to these, he will not see me – can get him to see the realities of the situation and get him to take the first step and negotiate.'

Arup was very upset by these accusations. Zunz, as he had so many times in the past, tried to pour oil on troubled waters. He wrote to Utzon: 'You and some of your supporters have been attacking and criticizing everyone who has faithfully supported you for many years.' He listed the client, Technical Advisory Panels, SOHEC, the RAIA and Arups among those who had been attacked.

'Is it not an impossible coincidence that they all become rogues and liars? …We are not perfect, when one deals with the most complex jobs imaginable some misunderstandings occur. However there is one thing we have not done. We have never been disloyal to you personally or to your ideal of the Opera House.'

Zunz added that Ryan's recollection of the conversation in which, he believed, Arup had suggested they supplant Utzon, was incorrect. The firm wanted to relieve itself of all the responsibilities other than structural and civil engineering, not take on more.

'One wonders whether you really want to finish the job – whether you've lost faith in your ability to meet the high standard you have set and whether you have built up the wall of half truths and fantasies to make excuses for your withdrawal. How else can one explain your leaving all of us who have worked hard and supported you in the lurch?'

The Opera House under construction 1966.

Lastly, Zunz raised the issue of Utzon's attacks on Arup himself: 'Your recent attitudes, statements and letters have been a savage blow to him personally. I wish you would stop and reconsider and look at the damage that has been done.'

On 10 May, Utzon wrote to his friend and supporter, Seidler: 'I hope you will understand that I had to get away from Sydney and also that I was unable to reveal my plans to you, as my solicitors had advised me above all to avoid meeting the press. Also, the atmosphere was unhealthy for the family, and anyhow I have to think of my other commitments now, but of course I haven't given up coming back to the Opera House.'

Povl Ahm, who had enjoyed a good relationship with Utzon throughout the project – Utzon designed his house in Harpenden, Hertfordshire – thought he could help. He went out to Sydney, but Utzon would not see him either. Ahm chased Utzon to Hawaii and on to Mexico City without success.

Several years later, Povl Ahm went to Hellebæk with Arup in the hope that he could affect a reconciliation. He left Arup in the Hellebæk Hotel over a cup of coffee and drove up to Utzon's home. He suggested to Utzon that the two should meet and make up:

'But Jørn wouldn't see him. It was most unfair – I am absolutely convinced that Ove had no idea of playing a greater role.'

Arup and Utzon did meet once more. In 1978, Utzon was presented with the Royal Gold Medal at the Royal Institute of British Architects headquarters in Portland Place, and Arup was in the audience. After the ceremony, the two shook hands and exchanged pleasantries. It was an emotional moment for those who had been through the tempestuous saga of the Sydney Opera House, but it was hardly a reconciliation.

CHAPTER 7
THE AFTERMATH

While the accusations flew around Sydney and resonated throughout the international architecture community, the Opera House site itself was relatively uneventful. Construction continued apace. The tile lids were going up at 20 a day. On 5 April 1966, the topmost segment of the tallest roof was lifted into place. Lewis was amazed to see Ryan, the former Minister of Public Works, showing a group of 70 people around the project. 'I don't think he visited the site more than twice a year when he was in charge,' Lewis wrote to Zunz in May.

The Government was faced with the problem of sorting out Utzon's fees, collecting and reviewing his drawings and getting the Architects' Panel of Hall, Todd and Littlemore started on Stage 3.

When Hall took on the job, he was under the impression he would be carrying out designs that were well defined. Utzon, however, believed no one could complete his work and that he would be called back once the new team had failed. 'The Architect's creation is largely in his own mind. No person can copy it.'

Charlie Weatherburn, as deputy Government Architect, was sent to Bennelong Point to review the drawings. When he went down to the site to pick up the drawings, 'the cupboard was almost bare'.

The two final drawings from the Utzon office showing crucial details of the proposed seating in the Major Hall were missing. These drawings, numbers 1383 and 1385 drawn at the end of 1965, are today available in the Mitchell Archives in Sydney and show a numbered seating plan with 2,518 seats in front of the orchestra, without using the closed off orchestra pit which would have allowed additional seats. Drawn ¼ scale they show seat spacing of 2ft 5in in the upper gallery and 2ft 7in in the lower auditorium.

On 31 May, Hall reported to the PWD that he was unable to find the seating layout drawings among those handed over by Utzon's office. He therefore drew the seats on negatives made from Utzon's original drawings, which showed the banking on which the seats would have been fixed. In this manner, he had worked out the total number of seats that could be accommodated based on two different spacing measurements. He arrived at the following conclusions:

'Row to row spacing dimensioned on his [Utzon's] drawings, viz. 2ft 5in in Gallery and 2ft 7in in Lower Auditorium, with 1ft 8in seat width (the width shown for the Minor Hall). On this basis approximately 2,250 seats are available.

Row to row spacing of 3ft 0in, with 1ft 8in seat width. On this basis there are approximately 1,800 seats.'

The new architectural team had carried out research in local Sydney theatres and concluded that the narrower spacing would not be comfortable. On a recent visit, Cremer and Gabler had reported that the row spacing at Bayreuth was 2ft 5in (736mm) and said that this was unsatisfactory.

The use of temporary seating over the orchestra pit for concerts would add a further 300 seats giving a total, at the narrower seat spacing, of 2,550 and 2,080 at the wider. Hall did not have access to the missing drawings nos. 1383 and 1385; if he had, he would have seen that with an extra 300 seats on the orchestra pit, Utzon was proposing a total of 2,818 seats but at the narrower, and generally unacceptable, seat spacing. So Utzon had squeezed in the requisite numbers but he had done so at the expense of comfort and of acoustic quality – both Nutsch and Cremer were unhappy about these numbers, feeling that the hall would be overloaded acoustically. The missing plans were put into store in Utzon's old office, which had been taken over by Bill Wheatland, together with some 5,000 sketches and drawings which were not handed over to the PWD. Prip-Buus wrote to his parents on 3 April 1966: 'they have only been given prints of old drawings relating to what has been built and nothing on all the new parts...'.

In 1972 when Wheatland was moving house, he and his wife felt it was time to return the drawings to their rightful owner, but Utzon insisted they be burnt. Wheatland refused to dispose of them in this way and suggested they should be placed in the Mitchell Library. After much debate Utzon agreed.

Weatherburn presented Hall's findings to the Technical Advisory Panel. 'The thing that really took the wind out of my sails,' Weatherburn remembers, 'is that Ashworth, who was the Professor of Architecture, and I think should have known better, asked me what I'd done with the 800 seats I'd lost. I said "I'm sorry, Professor," I was so taken aback, I said "you're on a false premise – you never had the 800 seats." "Oh". And that was the end of the meeting.'

A year later, Ashworth was to confide in Yuzo Mikami that he was convinced that Utzon was working on the basis of 2,800 seats. 'I just don't understand why Jørn didn't tell us. We might have been able to do something to help him if he had told us about the problem, but he didn't.' Ashworth later said that the Technical Advisory Panel had not seen any layouts of the Major Hall since 1963.

Hall was under Government orders to ensure that the Major Hall was suitable for use by the ABC, who were to be its principal users. On 7 June, Duckmanton, the ABC's general manager, wrote a letter, largely prepared by ABC engineer, Mehaffey, setting out the ABC's requirements:

Comfortable and well sighted seating for 2800.

Staging that would provide for a large choir surrounding the orchestra.

Acoustics appropriate to symphonic concerts with a reverberation time at middle frequencies in the region of 2.0 seconds when fully occupied, obtained without electronic assistance.

The Boston Symphony Hall, the Concertgebouw in Amsterdam, the old St Andrew's Hall, Glasgow, and the Grande Salle, Place des Arts, Montreal were given as examples of the character and diffusion of sound required, all classic 'shoebox' arrangements.

Desirable attributes were listed as: the exclusion of extraneous sounds and a quiet air conditioning system. The ABC also asked for a television control room, enclosed camera positions, parking and cable ducting for outside broadcast vans, a central apparatus room, 750 sq ft (70 sq m) of administration accommodation and a rehearsal space of not less than 210,000 cu ft (5,945 cu m). Unless these requirements were met, the ABC made it quite clear that they would prefer to remain in the Sydney Town Hall.

The architects were instructed by the Government to investigate the incorporation of the ABC's demands into the Opera House. It was clear to Hall that the Major Hall would have to be completely redesigned if it was to meet these requirements, although he was hampered by the lack of detailed drawings.

Commenting on the ABC's requirements, Cremer wrote from Berlin on 30 August: 'It is a pity that the ABC had not stated these requirements before the competition in 1957. This would have avoided the principal difficulties of the project which arise from the planning of two multipurpose halls of different capacity instead of planning one concert hall with a very large capacity and one auditorium with stage for opera and theatre with a smaller capacity.'

The inspection of the drawings left behind by Utzon raised the question of what he thought they would be used for. While Utzon said that his drawings of the glass walls and the auditoria ceilings were 'design' drawings that would be developed into 'shop' drawings by the specialist subcontractor for those items, he was claiming fees from the Government that would suggest he had completed the working drawings. Hall Todd and Littlemore, and Weatherburn, reported on their inspection of the drawings in June 1966:

'It was the understanding of the four signatories to this report that the drawings received would be working drawings for Stage Three of the project, i.e. that section of the work which is essentially architectural in character as opposed to Stage Two now under construction and which is essentially of a structural engineering nature.

'However it is noted from Mr Utzon's claim and the correspondence from the solicitors that the term working drawing or contract drawing has not been used on any occasion although the scale of fees charged does suggest that these documents were regarded by Mr Utzon as working drawings. The drawings reviewed are in a great number of cases classified as 'preliminary" and are in an unfinished state. This is particularly true of the Paving and Cladding drawings and those drawings dealing with the glass walls.

'At this stage it may be appropriate to define what we understand to be a "working drawing" and it could be said that a working drawing is one which when supplemented by a specification could be given to a job foreman or leading hand, following which the work can be placed in hand and completed with very little additional guidance from the Architect, except that which would flow from routine supervision. A detailed examination has been made of the 131 drawings received and we are unable to state that any of the 131 drawings received fall into the above category.'

Thirty years later, Farmer recalled what was discovered when the Government Architects had sight of the drawings from the Utzon office:

'The air conditioning plant was only just capable of serving the Major and

Minor Halls – below that level he [Utzon] apparently thought air conditioning unnecessary even though because of the few windows natural ventilation was impossible.

'Seating layout had not been drawn accurately and consequently audience capacity was unknown. As a result the acoustic design was not possible.

'Free standing decorative screens as shown in the "Unseen Utzon" models and drawings, if they ever could be built, were unsuitable acoustically.

'No contact had ever been made with the Theatre and Public Halls Act people or the Fire Brigade.

'There was no provision for proper stormwater drains or facilities for rodding them.

'There was no provision for cabling for power, audio, lighting, television and so on.

'No solution had been reached on construction of the huge glass walls – after nearly 10 years!

'When we took over we found no ⅛ scale general drawings of what had been done – our first act was to have surveyors measure up the inactive mass of concrete.'

Wheatland however is adamant that he had extensive discussions with Theatres and Public Halls Authorities in order to get them to accept Utzon's continental seating arrangements.

Farmer's comments are extreme. He was no fan of Utzon's. As a member of the Technical Advisory Panel, he had seen him operating over many years and had a very different view of what the practice of architecture is all about. He himself felt he could have as easily been an engineer as an architect and his main professional interest was in hospital architecture and equipment. On 1 April 1966, he wrote to Ian Lindsey, an architect in Scotland, saying: 'I do not regard Utzon as an architect, I regard him as an artist and sculptor of considerable merit.' The letter suggests that he regarded Utzon's concept as 'a gimmick'. Davis Hughes believed he would have been unable to confront Utzon in the way he did if Cobden Parkes had still been Government Architect.

Hall and several other members of the team undertook a tour of major concert halls and opera houses around the world to experience some of the older classic auditoria, as well as to see some of the newer buildings and to talk with their makers. This tour has been rather unfairly criticized by Philip

Drew, suggesting it was evidence of how little Hall knew about the subject. There was no secret of Hall's inexperience as far as concert halls were concerned – it was little different to Utzon's at the start of the project – and the grand tour of similar building types is standard practice among architects contemplating a major building, whether it is a theatre or an office block. Indeed, for Hall not to have made comparisons to international best practice would have been highly unprofessional.

Mehaffey also went on tour, looking at various projects of the acoustics consultant, Jordan – with which he was impressed – and meeting up with Cremer in Berlin in August. He did not get on with Cremer whom he found to be inflexible and lecturing. Cremer was an 'archetypal German professor' – he was prone to such remarks as, 'When I say what is right, I mean what is right – I am not expressing opinions.'

Mehaffey reported back to Duckmanton that Cremer maintained it was impossible to get more than 2,500 into the Major Hall, that it was impossible to include an organ and it would not be possible to get a reverberation time of 2.0 seconds. He could only manage 1.8 with difficulty and with the benefit of electronic assistance.

Mehaffey felt that the level of noise coming from the air conditioning would be acceptable, however – and in Mehaffey's eyes this utterly condemned the design – boat and tug sirens emanating from the harbour would still be audible in the Major Hall. In the epilogue to Michael Baume's 1967 book, *The Sydney Opera House Affair*, Hall wrote:

'It became increasingly clear that concerts and opera do not happen in the same sort of rooms. In a concert hall the orchestra should be in the same room as the audience; in an opera house, the proscenium separates the audience from the performers. They are different in acoustic quality, concerts needing longer reverberation time, and in their visual requirements. There are, especially in North America, a number of halls in which both are performed, but these are generally agreed to be not successful for both. I found almost complete agreement that opera and concerts are functions which do not combine well in one hall without loss of quality for concerts – Professor Cremer described it as a mistake in the original programme that it should have been required in Sydney – and that none of the best modern concert halls or opera houses is multi purpose: the best new concert hall, de Doelan in Rotterdam, is exclusively a concert hall, as is the Philharmonie in Berlin; the new Metropolitan Opera

Peter Hall with Willem Jordan.

House in New York and the new Berlin Opera are opera houses.'

Cremer's admission, after six years' work, that he could not put the two together satisfactorily was a major blow to the possibility of delivering a dual-purpose auditorium.

One of Hall's problems was the difficult relationship between the two teams of acoustics consultants. The prospect of getting a joint report out of them both was 'very remote'. The PWD report on Hall's travels noted:

'The German acoustics experts direct their efforts to the production of a kind of sound quality that is thought to be desirable in their country but which, as Mr Duckmanton has pointed out, is not wanted by the ABC, its orchestra or its audiences. Professor Cremer, I am convinced, tends to be inflexible on this point whereas Dr Jordan with his wider experience outside Europe, is quite prepared to endeavour to provide what the client requires and owing to this different philosophy on the art of acoustics it is impossible for them to collaborate. The time now appears to have arrived wherein it is essential to choose between them.'

While Hall held both acousticians in high esteem, he decided to select

Jordan for a number of reasons: Jordan would communicate in English while Cremer preferred to communicate in German; Jordan was used to working with Americans, and Hall believed that larger audiences in America had more in common with Sydney than the German experience; and, the ABC had a preference for Jordan's work. Certainly Jordan got on very well with Mehaffey and the two had conversations suggesting that Mehaffey might represent Jordan in Sydney. However, this proved impossible if Mehaffey was to stay with the ABC.

In any case, it was probable that Cremer would resign if it was decided to redesign the Major Hall and he had stated a number of times that he would do just that.

There were suggestions that, even at this late stage, an alternative site should be found in the centre of Sydney. Eiler Rasmussen wrote: 'The best thing would in my opinion be to stop all building when the shells are finished, and let Peter Hall or other persons build an unpretending new concert hall on another site far apart from Bennelong Point. It would leave the Utzon structure unspoiled and be much cheaper. It would also leave all possibilities open for the future...'

Hall mentioned this idea to Davis Hughes when they were on a plane journey together. 'Very interesting, but politically impossible,' said the Minister.

In December 1966, Hall Todd and Littlemore presented their report on the use of the various spaces in the Opera House, which stated that they could not make the idea of a dual–purpose hall work and suggested that the Major Hall should be a concert hall and that the Minor Hall should become the opera theatre. There followed a battle royal between the Elizabethan Theatre Trust, which sponsored opera in Australia, and the ABC.

The ABC was in a powerful position; if they didn't get their own way they could turn their back on Bennelong Point and continue to use Sydney Town Hall for concerts. They were committed to acoustics that would compare with the best concert halls in the world. They, and the Government at this stage, were risk averse – untried and untested solutions would not meet with approval.

Still, Utzon had not given up hope of returning. In February 1967, Lewis wrote to the London office to say that he had received a call from F Evers, a theatre correspondent for *The Australian*. According to Lewis, Evers told him that he had been speaking to Utzon who was willing to come back and to

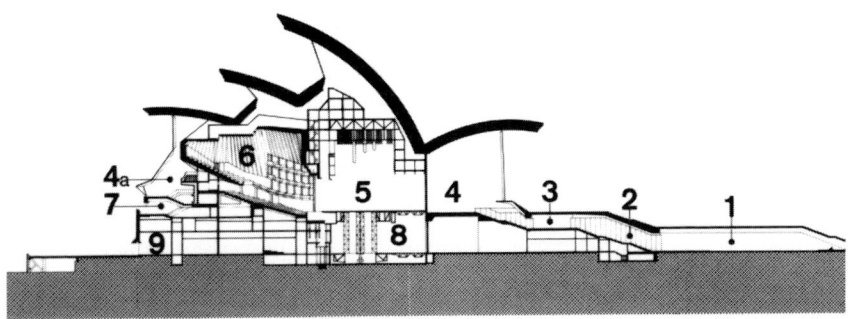

Both schemes

1 Concourse
2 Stairs
3 Box office foyer
4 South foyer bar area
4a North foyer bar area

Utzon's design (above)

5 Stage area
6 Auditorium
7 Dressing area
8 Stage machinery
9 Experimental theatre

Hall's design (below)

5 Organ
6 Concert hall
7 Rehearsal rooms
8 Studio
9 Drama theatre
10 Playhouse

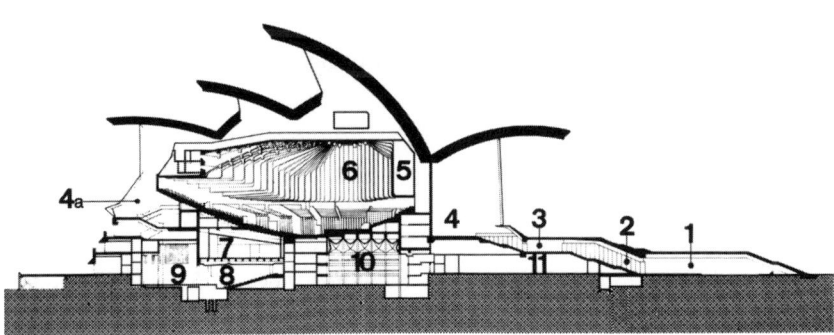

Cross sections of the Major Hall comparing Utzon's solution with Peter Hall's.

agree to a new form of organization and would work with Arups. He told Lewis that Utzon had said that he (Utzon) had been 'misinformed by his assistants' about the firm and sought the engineers' support. Lewis was noncommittal in his response.

Soon afterwards, *The Australian* published an interview with Utzon where he claimed to have solved all the building's problems and that he could put in the required number of seats. (In an article in *The Bulletin* in November 1968, Duek-Cohen suggests that Utzon's solution provided 2,800 seats in a dual-purpose hall with 2ft 10in spacing between seats.) Utzon said he was willing to go back to Australia and complete the building and that he was prepared to 'meet the Minister's demands for detailed cost estimates, a firm work schedule, a panel of architects to examine every item in the plans and report on its cost, feasibility and timing'.

The next day, Premier Askin was reported as saying that the Government had no intention of inviting Utzon back. Davis Hughes told the paper: 'There has been no approach to me by Mr Utzon and the question of his return does not arise. There is no situation which requires the attention of Mr Utzon. The panel is very competent to deal with any requirements of the client for the completion of the Opera House.'

Davis Hughes had made up his mind. The following month he announced that he was supporting the ABC's position – the Major Hall would be a concert hall, opera would be relegated to the Minor Hall; the Major Hall stage machinery would be scrapped – at a cost of A\$3million – and the rehearsal room for the orchestra placed in the space beneath the stage that would have housed the now redundant machinery. The experimental theatre was now to be used for drama.

Yuzo Mikami visited Sydney to see the completion of Stage 2 in February 1967 when the last shell lid was dropped into place, and tried to persuade Hall to design a convertible hall as opposed to the multi-purpose hall which Utzon had been persevering with. With the multi-purpose hall in concert mode, the orchestra is positioned at the front of the stage which means that it is almost impossible to increase the number of seats in the main body of the hall. And even if it was possible, the reverberation time is reduced, just the opposite of what is required. With a convertible hall, where adjustable ceiling systems allow the volume of the space to be changed, the orchestra can be moved to the rear of the room thus allowing more seats with the appropriate volume and reverberation times.

Mikami was upset that Hall's rearrangement fundamentally damaged Utzon's original concept. If the allocation of spaces remained unchanged, at least Hall would be able to build the Minor Hall as Utzon intended. Mikami asked Arups to allow him some time to study the concept of a convertible hall. After a study of several weeks, he came to the firm conclusion that it was perfectly feasible to design a convertible hall for the Major Hall obtaining a seating capacity of 2,807 for concerts and 1,811 for opera with 3ft 4in (1010mm) spacing between rows. However, he did add the caveat that a hall of that type had never been built before and that the technical difficulties of the demountable parts were very great. Almost 20 years later, Mikami was able to illustrate the viability of the convertible hall when he designed the Orchard Hall in Tokyo using three telescoping shells which, when the hall is in opera mode, are located at the back of the stage. For concerts, they move forward on rails to form a single large shell which encloses the orchestra and reflects sound into the main auditorium. The acoustics are excellent but, crucially, the hall is small and holds less than 2,000 people.

On 28 March 1967, Ove Arup wrote to Davis Hughes: 'I understand that your Government has now finally decided to abandon the idea of using the Major Hall for opera. It is a very dramatic – almost one might say, tragic – decision because it makes a nonsense of the whole form of the shells, which were meant to house the stage tower.'

The decision to reallocate the functions of the building had a major impact on the design and construction programme. Although the roof structure was completed a year after Utzon's departure, it was not until 1969 that work was to begin on Stage 3.

As his interior layout was finally consigned to the bin, Utzon made one last attempt to return. On 14 September 1967, Hall had a telephone conversation with Utzon in which they discussed his participation in the partnership. Hall's note of the conversation reads: 'Would Mick Lewis be all right? I said that I thought that if the Government would agree that Utzon should work with us, that I was sure that Mick would accept that. I told him that Ove Arup himself was in favour of having him back and that he should talk to Ove about this. He said he thought that was good news.'

Then, in February the next year, a public meeting was held in Sydney Town Hall called by the Bring Back Utzon campaigners, with Elias Duek-Cohen and former Minister Ryan among the speakers. A tape recording of Utzon made two weeks earlier in Hellebæk was played in which he stressed his enthusiasm for returning to Sydney to finish the building. He said that he had solved the problems of the Major Hall as a multi-purpose hall '...in comfortable seats as the government wanted'.

Interviewed on ABC's *This Day To-night* on 28 February 1968, he was asked whether he would insist on being the controlling architect if he was brought back. He replied, 'No, I would like to collaborate so that the team could get the best result from a team work.' He was asked about his conversations with Hall and replied, 'Mr Hall was actually very eager for me to come back, and he is a professional man, as a colleague of me [sic], he expressed that I should be fulfilling my work, and he would like to collaborate with me to that extent.'

The Government showed little interest in the possibility of Utzon returning and work carried on under Hall Todd and Littlemore, despite the fact that the cost estimates had now risen to A$85million. To Utzon, who had fended off the Government over rising costs for years, the news that they had agreed to a cost that was four times his last estimate was confirmation that he had been unjustly treated.

One of the most intractable problems at this time was the design of the glass walls. Fitting such large areas of glass into an existing structure with conflicting geometries at each edge, while maintaining the fundamental elements of Utzon's approach, was a formidable task and took four years to solve. Arups engineer, John Nutt, wrote a report on the selection of materials for the mullions of the glass walls and reiterated the criticisms of plywood he had made previously and which manufacturer Symonds had failed to answer. Nutt was concerned about water absorption and weathering, and the variable penetration of preservatives:

'No definite information on the effectiveness of preserving treatments has been established and, although from April 1962 we repeatedly asked Mr Utzon for durability tests to be carried out, no such testing programme has been initiated.'

Nutt also suggested that there was considerable doubt over the durability of bronze-covered plywood – a major element of the Utzon design – Nutt said it was essential that durability tests were initiated on any plywood proposals and that these tests would take at least two years. The chances of the Government agreeing to such a delay was negligible.

Wheatland never had any doubt about the longevity of metal reinforced and clad plywood, pointing out the success of the roof of the Myer Music

Bowl in Melbourne. The Bowl, built in 1959, consists of a sandwich of ply and aluminium (Alumply) suspended on cables. The ply was replaced in 2001 when the building was refurbished by Gregory Burgess Architects. Burgess' consultants, Arup Facade, recommended that Alumply was still the most appropriate material.

In any case, the possibility of pursuing plywood options for the walls as well as the auditoria ceilings was destroyed when the Receiver Manager of Ralph Symonds told Lionel Todd that the company was withdrawing from all commitments and would accept no responsibilities for any information or assurances the company had given to Utzon.

At the time of his resignation, Utzon was considering a design for the glass walls using substantial plywood mullions, some as deep as 9ft 10in (3m) to cater for the curves set up by the ribs. The glass was to be fixed at the leading edge of one mullion and to the rear edge of the next in order to allow it to follow the shape of the roof in plan. Not only did this give the impression of a virtually solid wall when viewed from the side, it also presented a large area of wind resistance in the east-west direction – an important factor in an open location like Bennelong Point. The mullions also obscured east-west views from the interior.

Numerous other materials had been considered – laminated timber, steel, stainless steel, bronze and aluminium – but Nutt recommended concrete, which was durable, easily formed into complex shapes and a material with which Arups were familiar. The chief disadvantage of concrete mullions, unlike plywood, was that they could not be hung from the shells. They would need to be supported from below and merely stabilized by the shells.

Some prototype mullions were made and erected under the shells. The results were not a great success. Visually they looked as though they were supporting the shells – in contrast to Utzon's concept where he envisaged the glass walls hanging from the shells. Helge Hjertholm, who had worked on the project in Hellebæk, visited Sydney and saw the prototypes. Appalled, he wrote to Arup pleading for him to intervene.

However, Hjertholm was not alone in finding them visually unacceptable and there were concerns about the weight of the mullions, so the concrete scheme was scrapped.

Yuzo Mikami – as one of the closest links with Utzon available to the architects – wrote a letter to Hall outlining the philosophy of the glass walls. He stressed the need to create a light, hanging feeling with maximum

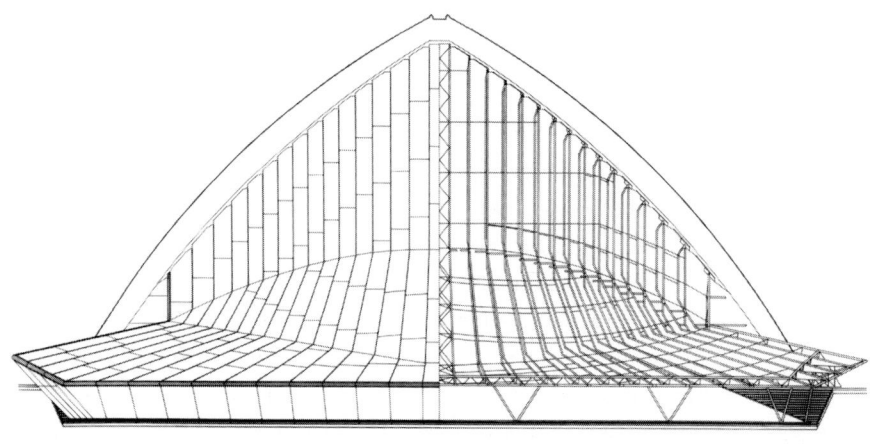

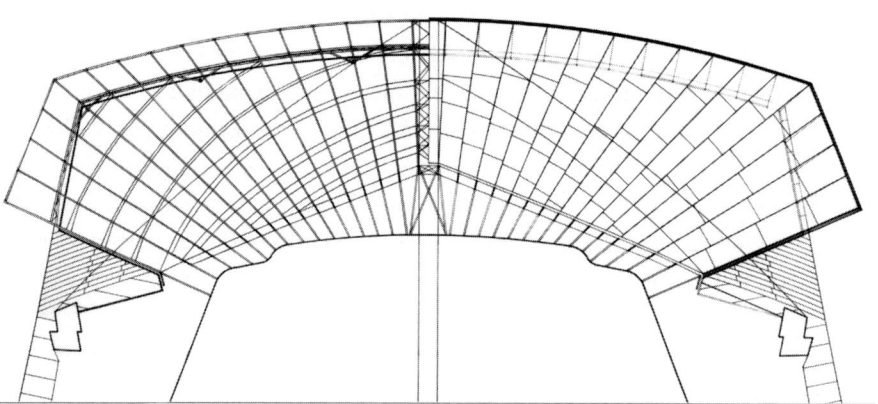

The glass walls designed by Peter Hall and Arups. The 'tusks' rather unsatisfactorily cut off the base of the shells before they meet the podium.

transparency. The sectional dimensions of the mullions should be as small as possible and should not be made of concrete. They should seem to hang from the shells and should be dark in colour to contrast with the shells and tiles. He also recommended as many doors as practically possible in the glazing surrounding the circulation spaces so that patrons could 'freely go out of the enclosed space and enjoy the fresh air'.

In the end, steel was chosen as the structural material because of its high strength and stiffness in relation to its weight, although it brought with it formidable weathering and durability problems in the salty harbour environment. The planar glazing with minimal external mullions and internal steel structure set back from the glass that was developed for the walls was the precursor of a style of enclosure that has now become commonplace; but at that time it pushed the boundaries of contemporary technology to the limit. The sheets of glass were to be supported along their vertical edges with the horizontal joints sealed with silicone rubber, a form of sealant that was in its infancy and required substantial research to ascertain its suitability and longevity. The engineers developed a standard mullion constructed of two parallel tubes separated by a plate web to support the glass from behind.

In the Design Principles prepared in 2000, Utzon accepts that the glass walls as built are 'in family with the glass wall we arrived at with its feeling of its hanging from the shell'. Adding that, 'At the last meeting I had with the engineer from Ove Arup's firm, Mick Lewis, I handed over the drawings for mullions made of twin pipes with a distance between them, which the sketches will show, which is somewhat similar to the solution which had been used. And upon seeing this Mick Lewis said, "Well now I can make the glass wall".'

Lewis, however, cannot recall such a conversation taking place. David Croft, the Arups engineer whose job it was to work out the glass walls, remembers that it was Nutt who came up with the idea of two tubes separated by a steel plate. What is apparent is that Utzon had considered the use of steel. At the site meeting between architects and engineers held on 23 December 1965, the glass walls were discussed:

'SOH No 1388 shows a mullion containing a steel girder. The architect explained that he did not have in mind any change from the plywood scheme but that he would like the engineer to advise him on the dimensions of the steel mullions in order to have a better understanding of the forces at work in the mullions.'

Utzon was represented by three of his architects, but was not present at the meeting.

Croft arrived from London in 1967, when the cladding of the podium walls and the paving were almost complete, and the empty gothic monolith stood proud and lonely on its harbour promontory. 'It was a magnificent structure, like a cathedral,' Croft recalls. Jim Anderson from Hall's office had done a lot of work on the shape of the glazing and Croft set to calculating the structure. Relationships between him and Anderson became strained as they argued about the best way to solve the difficult 'tusks' that wrap around the base of the north facades and how the glass was to be supported. Anderson wanted to support the glass on 6in (150mm) circular pads fixed to the glass sheets. The arguments led to a 'one year stand off' as different solutions were batted between the teams. Croft was one of Arups' most brilliant engineers; he excelled creatively and analytically, but was not quite so effective in the personal relations department.

When Zunz visited Sydney in 1968, Hall and Croft were hardly talking. After Zunz 'banged their heads together' work continued, although not without argument. In what became nicknamed the 'Battle of the Blobs', Croft voiced his dislike of the circular pads because of the stresses they placed on the glass. While such pads are a common enough feature in glazing today, they are generally used on vertical walls; however, the geometry of the Opera House was such that, in some cases, the glazing is almost horizontal. Arup did not like the look of them and wrote to Hall telling him so. Hall defended his design saying that he didn't want to have a 'metal curtain wall' but a finish that was 'shiny and crystalline'.

The strained relationship between Croft and Anderson was brought to an abrupt end in October 1969 when the whole of the architect's glass wall team resigned, including Anderson. It was a bad time for Hall; he was having personal problems – he had just divorced his wife – and Arups felt that he was not leading the team as a design architect should and was giving way to the PWD and his non-design partners on a number of crucial issues. He was better at analysis than taking decisions. Numerous times the engineers agreed a decision with Hall only to have it overturned once he had reported back to his partners or the PWD. The partnership of Hall, Todd and Littlemore had been a shotgun marriage and was not a happy relationship. The situation deteriorated to such a low ebb that, at one point, Ove Arup wanted to resign from the job altogether. He had several attempts at drafting a letter to Davis Hughes. In October 1969, he wrote:

'...we can see no prospect of a happy conclusion with the present team in charge.

'Our engineers who have worked up to eight years on the glass walls simply refuse to have anything to do with the job.

'To employ three government employees to form a firm and complete the world's most difficult building was a gamble which could not be expected to succeed.'

In his November draft of the letter, he added, 'The Opera House has become a millstone around our neck. We would dearly like to get rid of it or at least ease the burden.'

Lewis was more cautious. He replied to Arup that resignation 'is an act which I cannot contemplate at this late hour.' He thought, however, that some letter expressing the firm's dissatisfaction should be placed on record.

Two particular items were frustrating the engineers – the proposal for an escalator on the front steps leading up to the building, and a decision by Davis Hughes to seek a private operator for a multistorey car park to serve the Opera House. There was no specified site, but the engineers feared it could be close enough to the Opera House to have a serious effect on Utzon's architectural concept for the exterior of the building. Davis Hughes complained that there was no money in the budget for the car park and a private operator was the only solution. For the first time the costs of the Opera House had outstripped the income from the lottery and the PWD was forced to look to bridging finance to carry the project forward. The brief to potential operators proposed by the Minister was so open that it was feasible that they could end up with a multistorey car park located anywhere between the Cahill Expressway and the Opera House steps. As to the escalator, this had been proposed to counteract considerable criticism that there was no mechanical means to assist disabled visitors to get into the building. Zunz felt that an escalator would do little to assist the elderly and infirm, but would certainly destroy Utzon's concept of the Mayan plateau. Even today, visitors who have difficulty with stairs are advised to book seats in the lower areas of the two main auditoria. They are guided into the service area where they can take a lift to the stalls.

Davis Hughes had visited London towards the end of 1969 and had discussed at length with Arups the car park and the escalators. Arups thought they had convinced the Minister of the inappropriateness of the proposals and were surprised and dismayed to discover that immediately on his return to Australia, Davis Hughes instructed the architects to proceed with the escalators.

Frustrated, Ove Arup wrote to Davis Hughes in January 1970 to reiterate the firm's views on the two issues. 'To strive for perfection to the tune of A$85million and then spoil the whole thing in order to save A$3million is, we think, indefensible.' It was written as an open letter and Arup informed the Minister that he reserved the right to publish it and give it to the press.

Davis Hughes' reply in February said that the Government would probably not go ahead with the escalators, but he was not prepared to concede on the matter of the car park.

The Minister's implacable views on the matter finally drove even Lewis to contemplate withdrawing from the Opera House. He met with Davis Hughes to tell him that Arups had decided to take a stand on the car park proposals and presented the firm's demands: that the car park should not be above ground if it was to the north of Circular Quay, that it should be within easy walking distance and it should house a minimum of 1,000 cars. He wrote to Davis Hughes afterwards:

'We said to you at the meeting that we felt sufficiently strongly on the issue that if the criteria outlined above could not or would not be met we would tender our resignation from the job.'

In the event, Davis Hughes did not proceed with the multistorey car park, but the incident illustrates Arup's continuing commitment to protecting the fundamental architectural qualities of Utzon's concept.

There was still no car park for the Opera House when it opened in 1973. Plans to excavate beneath the Royal Botanic Gardens were foiled by the Building Labourers Federation, led by the celebrated activist Jack Mundey, who placed a Green Ban on the project because it would have interfered with the root system of the ancient Moreton Bay Fig trees above.

The glass walls were finally completed in 1971, rendering the building weatherproof and allowing the long awaited construction of the interior to commence.

Hall has been treated less than fairly in the criticisms of his work at the Opera House. The quality of his interiors for the Concert Hall and Opera Theatre bear comparison with other, similar halls around the world. The sweeping striated plywood of the Concert Hall is not out of context with

Utzon's architecture while the acoustics were, at the time of the opening, commended as being of the highest quality. 'Second to none' was Joan Sutherland's comment. Ted Farmer recalled how Yehudi Menuhin played a Bach unaccompanied partita in the Concert Hall and told Hall and Farmer 'This is the best concert hall I've ever played in', to their great relief. The fact that attitudes to acoustics have moved on and that the Concert Hall today has to cope with a wider range of events than anticipated should not detract from Hall's and Jordan's achievement. But in the end Hall only managed to fit 2,679 seats into the Concert Hall, 121 short of target, including 579 behind the orchestra, the spacing between seat rows being 2ft 11ins (889mm).

The more sombre interior of the Opera Theatre, with its angular balconies and vaulted ceilings, is an elegant play on the architectural elements of the roof shells which focuses the viewers' attention onto the stage area. As an approach it conflicts, however, with Utzon's idea of progressing through the building where 'as you enter, the hall explodes into a very rich expression of colours'.

The undersized orchestra pit and difficulties such as, according to Ava Hubble the SOH Press Officer at the time of the opening, 'the 60-strong chorus for the performance of War and Peace ...lined up for rehearsals in a crocodile that stretched from the wings, down a passageway and flight of steps into the green room' were problems set in concrete when Stage 1 was built.

The building was opened on 20 October 1973 by Queen Elizabeth II with a performance of Beethoven's Ninth Symphony, a specially commissioned fanfare and Jubugalee (another name for Bennelong), a piece by the Australian composer, John Antill. Utzon was invited to the ceremony but did not attend.

However, the Opera House was not yet fully complete. By a strange twist of fate, the story of the construction of the organ reflects many of the characteristics and dramas of the construction of the building itself. The central figure of this story was Ronald Sharp, a self-taught organ-builder; he was, like Utzon, a perfectionist and a man to whom the quality of the end product was of greater importance than cost and time. His unconventional approach was seen by his antagonists as incompetence and by his supporters as a sign of his genius. The original cost of the organ was estimated at A$400,000; the final bill was A$1.2million and it was not completed until 1979, four years behind schedule. The English organist, Peter Hurford,

Hall's concert hall.

advised the Opera House Organ Committee and was a great supporter of Sharp. 'He is very difficult to work with, this is true,' according to Hurford, but 'the integrity of his overall design is perhaps worth the problems one encounters on the way.'

The selection of organ-builder was made by the Organ Committee, chaired by Sir Bernard Heinze and including Warwick Mehaffey who, as well as working for the ABC, was also a director of the Organ Institute of Sydney, a member of the Organ Society of Sydney and had, coincidentally, played the organ in the Sydney Town Hall on the occasion of Utzon's first visit in 1958.

There were several campaigns to remove Sharp from the commission, and when he was unable to complete the organ by 1980, the PWD insisted that he accept the assistance of another organ-builder. The Austrian firm of Gregor Hradetzky helped Sharp complete the job. Despite his bitter disappointment and the huge pressures upon him, Sharp, unlike Utzon, stayed on to see his masterwork – the largest mechanical-action organ in the world – completed. He was present to hear the Melbourne organist, Douglas Lawrence, launch the inaugural concerts on 7 June 1979 with Mozart's Fantasia in F and Bach's Toccata and Fugue in D minor.

The leader in the *Sydney Morning Herald* following the inaugural recital read:

'People are often suspicious of dreamers. We feel safer with tenders, committees, organisations. If our dreamer takes too long to deliver the goods, or costs us too much money, we become harshly critical. We drove Jørn Utzon from the Opera House. We came perilously close to doing the same thing to Ronald Sharp.'

CHAPTER 8
ARS LONGA, VITA BREVIS

The 'Unseen Utzon' exhibition in 1995 gave new heart to the 'Bring Back Utzon' campaign. Included in the show were some of Utzon's original drawings of the interiors. The implication was that if these drawings had been 'seen' then Utzon's interiors could have been completed. Although the drawings were unseen as far as the general public was concerned, some of them had certainly been seen by Peter Hall in 1966.

Also in the exhibition were computer-generated images created by Philip Nobis, a postgraduate student at Sydney University of Technology, which suggested Utzon's designs for the halls could be built, leading Duek Cohen and others to suggest that the interiors designed by Hall be replaced with Utzon's sweeping plywood ceilings and radial layouts. The exhibition gave new impetus to the debate on Utzon's interiors and was one of the reasons behind the decision in 1999 by the Opera House Trust to appoint Utzon as a consultant to prepare his statement of Design Principles in conjunction with the Sydney architect Richard Johnson, with the aim of ensuring that future changes to the building should, according to the Sydney Opera House Trust, reflect 'the integrity of Jørn Utzon's vision for the building'. In the years since the resignation, Utzon's view of Arup has mellowed. In the Principles he writes: '…I was pushed aside as architect for the job. Luckily Ove Arup stayed on the job; otherwise it would never have been completed.'

In May 2002, the NSW Premier, Bob Carr, announced the allocation of A$45million for major improvements to the Opera House, which involved: the enlargement of the orchestra pit and refurbishment of the auditorium of the Opera Theatre; providing the infrastructure for the use of the forecourt area as a sixth venue; improvements to the acoustics of the Concert Hall; and, refurbishing the Western Broadwalk, the foyer and the Reception Hall. Coincidentally, the name of the project manager for the initial round of works was David Hughes.

Newspaper reports, TV programmes and publications about the Opera House appearing in recent years have increasingly reflected the pro-Utzon line. Typically, the *Australian Daily Telegraph* of 10 July 2002 introduced its article, 'Utzon return something to sing about', with the words, 'Architect Jørn Utzon was hounded out of Sydney nearly four decades ago by that disgracefully Philistine vandal Davis Hughes, Public Works Minister in the Askin Government.' Articles invariably contain a potted history that runs something like this: 'Utzon designed a remarkable roof which was so complex that the engineers were unable to work out how to build it. In a eureka moment Utzon solved the structural problems for them. As the project continued, Utzon was blamed for increases of cost which were not of his making, but nevertheless philistine politicians, unwilling or unable to recognize Utzon's genius and with the collusion of the engineers, forced him to resign. The completed building is a shadow of that proposed by Utzon who had, in fact solved all the problems at the time of his resignation.'

Such analyses led Zunz to write to Mikami in 1999, 'History is being rewritten.' He felt that Utzon's supporters took the view that, 'if facts and reality get in the way then spin a few well chosen sentences and create a fog of lies and half truths.'

The previous chapters have pieced together what happened from contemporary reports, minutes, letters and eye witness accounts. The story sheds light on many of the contentious issues that make up the Sydney Opera House saga and highlights the mounting pressures that were affecting Utzon in the final months.

Architecture at the edge of the possible inevitably generates difficulties of timing, of technology, of cost, and stretches the patience and relationships of those involved. The building of Brunelleschi's fifteenth-century dome for Florence Cathedral, still the largest masonry dome in existence, contains striking resonance with the story of the Opera House. It was the result of a competition and the local unsuccessful competitor, Lorenzo Ghiberti, was a continual critic of Brunelleschi's plans. The dome used previously untried construction techniques; both the design of massive hoists to haul the 1,700lb sandstone blocks up into the cupola and Brunelleschi's construction techniques, which avoided the need for scaffolding beneath the dome, bear comparison with Corbet Gore's erection arches and prestressing techniques. Brunelleschi, like Utzon, never saw his masterwork completed.

He died soon after the cupola was topped out but before the lantern was put into place at the summit.

There are also comparisons to be drawn with the Los Angeles Disney Concert Hall designed by Frank Gehry. Even in the early 1990s – more than 30 years after the design of the Sydney shells – Gehry did not have ready access to computers large enough to calculate and prepare the drawings for the complex structural and cutting patterns of his free flowing forms. Costs escalated and the project temporarily collapsed. It was revived in 1997 and to cut costs a firm of executive architects were appointed causing Gehry to hand in his resignation. He was only willing to stay on the job after the daughter of Walt Disney provided an additional US$14 million to pay for Gehry's office to do the working drawings.

The question is, did Utzon want to see his building completed strongly enough? Did the pressures become so great that resignation was the only escape?

The ability to carry an idea through from conception to completion, while all the time maintaining its essence, is the hallmark of a great artist in any discipline. But while painters, sculptors and even composers have few constraints on their work, architects face a tougher regime if they are to see their ideas and drawn concepts become functioning buildings.

The early stage of a design is the closest the architect gets to having the freedom of the artist – he must address certain aspects of function, but does not yet have to deal with planners, contractors or to keep the rain out. Drawings allow the architect to work through concepts, develop ideas and to illustrate an approach without necessarily observing the practicalities that may emerge later in the process.

Architects often develop ideas with little prospect or intention of actual construction. Neither Sir John Soane's designs for triumphal bridges in the 1770s nor Archigram's Plug-In City of 1963 were drawn with the idea that they would ever be built; these exercises developed the architects' own ideas, as well as the viewers' understanding of them, and were hugely influential. Architects frequently use competitions as a vehicle for such investigations. Competitions have the advantage of defining some of the practicalities involved in architectural design with real briefs and constraints. While most architects enter competitions with the clear intent of winning them, much of their enthusiasm stems from the chance to stretch their architectural muscles, to excite their teams and to move ideas along. This, to some extent, explains why so many man-hours are spent on the long-shot of winning an open competition where the odds are frequently several hundred to one.

Utzon liked entering competitions; they were one of the ways he investigated architectural ideas. According to Siegfried Giedion, he was very surprised when he won the Sydney Opera House competition. He used the Opera House brief to develop his ideas relating to Mayan architecture, the cloud-like shells and his brilliant, but flawed, plan. The idea was simple, but not enough thought had been put into how it would work, how it would be built, whether it could contain the required activities. The competition entry did not address any of the ideas of construction, geometry or prefabrication that consumed Utzon in the later years of the project.

The fact that the structure of the competition-winning entry was virtually impossible to build suggests that Utzon was more interested in working through the theoretical rather than the practical aspects of his design.

Most architects want to see their designs built; they are driven by the desire to see their drawings and concepts become real forms and usable spaces; did Utzon lack this particular part of the architectural psyche or was he more content with ideas and drawings? As Michael Webb, member of the Archigram Group – who famously never carried out a major built project – said when he collected the group's Royal Gold Medal in 2002, 'The problem with the reality of building is that you lose that initial magic.' In February/March 1962, Utzon had said to Zunz as they lay on a beach in Hawaii that he did not care whether the job was cancelled as he had 'solved all the problems'. He repeated this comment to Zunz in August of that year. Even today, in his advancing years, he has no desire to see the building in the flesh, although he tells curious Sydney journalists that he sees it in his mind every night. The building of the mind can be a perfect building.

Utzon, nevertheless, struggled for nine years to see his ideas become concrete. What forced him to jeopardize his position and his professional reputation when he did? The most pressing was his lack of money, but at the time of his resignation, a whole range of issues was closing in on him. In the version of events related by Richard Weston in his book *Utzon* – the only book about the architect produced with Utzon's input and cooperation – the architect became aware of the Government's disaffection when, in a bizarre scene that could come straight from a spy movie, Utzon received a telephone call telling him to go to the gates of the Opera House site where a man in a green car would be waiting for him. It turned out to be former Minister of

Public Works, Norman Ryan. It was clear to Utzon that Ryan did not want to be recognized. The ex-Minister then warned Utzon that the Government intended to make a scapegoat of him, that he would support Utzon and that he was aware that Utzon was doing everything he could to complete the project. Ryan was a staunch supporter of Utzon. He had promised Cahill before he died that he would see the project through. However he was under great pressure from his own party to bring the Opera House under control and it was Ryan who, as minister, first put pressure on Utzon with the appointment of Wood – the source of many of the architect's problems with the PWD.

Weston also suggests that the architects were making good progress on the design during 1965, yet the evidence of site meetings, minutes and drawings is that there was little progress on the glass walls or on the accommodation in the Major Hall – the latter having reached an almost total impasse and, according to Cremer, presented insurmountable difficulties for an audience of 2,800. The 'Unseen Utzon' exhibition of 1994 showed nothing that fundamentally changed the 1966 position.

In Weston's version, Utzon's letter following the fateful meeting with Davis Hughes on 28 February was no more than a 'withdrawal', that he advised his staff not to look for other work because he expected to be asked to return. If so, it was a strategy that went horribly wrong.

The use of threats of resignation is a time-honoured tactic for improving one's position in a negotiation. However, it is only effective when the person threatening to resign is in a position of strength. Utzon believed he was. He was convinced that only he could complete the design of the Opera House; it was his personal vision, it was in his mind. Davis Hughes had a different agenda. His priorities were to get the project under control; he had little sympathy for the finer points of Utzon's architectural sensibilities. He once described Utzon's red and gold interior for the Major Hall as looking like a 'Paris boudoir'.

It is hardly surprising that Hughes thought Utzon meant to resign. Talk of resignation was in the air. It is clear from Prip-Buus' diary that, during the previous year, the subject was regularly discussed. Utzon had told Lewis in advance that he intended to resign; Lewis advised him against it, telling him: 'You must never resign. Resigning solves nothing.' Lewis reminded him that he had been appointed by Act of Parliament, which would have made it very difficult for Davis Hughes to sack him. Lewis told Arup of

Utzon's threat and Arup wrote to Utzon in February 1966 warning him against such precipitate action. 'I heard you mentioned the possibility of resigning from the job if the clients did not see eye to eye with you. I don't suppose this was meant seriously, but just in case you are playing with the idea I should like, as a friend, to warn you against it.

'As I see it, if you resign all is lost. It would be a most dangerous thing even to hint at it. If you want just to use it as a threat you must first be quite sure that it will not be accepted. And can you be so absolutely sure?'

But the letter arrived after Utzon's fateful meeting with Davis Hughes.

Month on month, Utzon had become increasingly entangled in the problems of the Opera House; political, administrative, financial, technical and architectural. It was little wonder he wanted to give up.

The Sydney Opera House Executive Committee, the client for the first six years of the project, had been replaced by the Government's Public Works Department. SOHEC was a well-meaning group who, individually, were leaders in their field; but together they were hopelessly inadequate to the task of controlling a major building project. They failed to define the brief at the beginning and they continually changed their minds. But in many ways they suited Utzon; he was a brilliant and charming presenter and he had the committee in his thrall. Lewis recalls attending a SOHEC meeting where Utzon told them confidently he could include 2,800 seats in the Major Hall. Lewis counted the seats on the drawing and it was more like 1,900. Arup, in a written commentary on the affair, said, 'What we disliked later on was the whole policy of concealment of the true position from the public, the Government and the Technical Advisory Panel even, in order to put a brave face on the whole affair.'

When Minister Ryan started to take control and assume the role of client, Utzon's charm had less effect. Utzon's client was no longer a friendly and supportive committee who paid him the respect he felt he deserved and money when he wanted it, but a critical and, in some cases, cynical group with whom he was out of step.

Utzon did not get on with Wood, who was hardly the sort of character to ingratiate himself with the Utzon camp. An administrative architect rather than a designer, he was continually concocting schemes whereby he could pin down the butterfly creativity of the charismatic Dane. Described by Lewis as 'aged, tiresome and a pain', Wood reported to Farmer, the Government Architect who led a well-respected department but was sceptical of Utzon's architectural approach. The down-to-earth Government architects, used to highly structured and conventional working procedures, found Utzon's foreign and radical approach difficult to deal with.

Increasingly vociferous criticisms of the cost of the Opera House added to Utzon's woes. Blame for the ever-escalating estimates could only partly be laid at Utzon's door: hasty calculations right at the start based on the incomplete competition scheme – SOHEC's vacillations, the premature start on site, the need to announce costs before they were known, the complexity of construction – all these factors contributed to a belief by the media and among politicians that the scheme was out of control. When it became an issue in the 1965 election, it was inevitable that whichever party won, the appointed Minister for Public Works would be under pressure to 'do something' about it. In light of the fact that the Public Lottery was in credit for the whole time that Utzon was in charge, this might be seen as an unnecessary interference by the politicians; but the Sydney Opera House Act deemed that increases in costs had to be ratified by Parliament and neither Ryan nor Davis Hughes were keen to go back to the legislative assembly to ask for more money.

From 1964 onwards, Utzon's relations with the Government were becoming increasingly tense and less pleasant. The final straw was the instigation of Wood's 'cheque book control' in late 1965 when Davis Hughes decreed that Utzon would be paid at a rate based on the amount of work that had been done and not, as had happened under SOHEC, on the basis of how much he needed to run the office. Payment for work done is not an unusual method of remunerating architects, but the change led to delays in payment by the Government which created a cash crisis in Utzon's office exacerbated by a substantial tax bill from the Commonwealth Tax Office. Utzon's financial problems threatened his ability to stay in Australia.

Life in the Antipodes was not always amenable. Neither architects nor engineers held the status that they did in Denmark – a trait inherited from the British. Povl Ahm recalls how shocked he was when he arrived in London from Denmark to discover the comparatively low esteem in which engineers were held in England. The Danish-ness of Utzon is an important element in the story. His relationship with Arup was founded on their common nationality and language. Schooled in the heavily craft-orientated traditions of Danish architecture, Utzon was disdainful of the quality of workmanship he found in Australia and looked to factory-based production methods to

View of the Opera House from the north looking toward the city centre.

circumvent the problem. Prip-Buus' letters from Sydney to his parents are a catalogue of complaints about everything Australian, from spiders to health care. The brash and bustling Sydney of the 1960s was a long way from the calm vastness of Utzon's beloved beech forests of Hellebæk and the raw clarity of the Oresund heaped with history and legend. Growing antagonism from his client, consultants and the media could not have helped his peace of mind. His move to Palm Beach, a peninsula to the north of the city, attempted to recreate the quiet creative environment of the Danish studio; but outside the gates, the wolves circled. The press was always ready to have a go and would rarely fail to obtain a critical quote from the disgruntled Walter Bunning.

Press relations on the Opera House were handled appallingly badly by the Government and Utzon seemed content to let them deal with public announcements. He was a keen publicist, but preferred the certainties of the architectural press, particularly the Italian architecture periodical, *Zodiac*, in which he was provided with a comprehensive platform for his theories and designs. The magazine was an important conduit for new architectural ideas in the 1960s. Coincidentally, it had been launched in 1957, when Utzon won the Opera House competition, and ceased publication the year the building opened, 1973.

Utzon turned down Ron Gilling's offer to produce a booklet which might have helped to explain what was going on at Bennelong Point from an architectural perspective.

Working in Palm Beach, with no telephone and making the 25 mile journey into Sydney twice a week, was hardly the most efficient *modus operandi* for a project of this scale. Utzon worked by producing freehand sketches which he then passed on to assistants to draw up. In Hellebæk, he could work at home and walk along the beach to the office, sometimes stopping for a swim on the way; in Sydney, he sketched in Palm Beach while the majority of architects remained on the site. There was clearly a limit to the amount of work that could be carried out in this manner and a limit to the number of assistants who could be controlled. Mikami suggests that at Hellebæk the maximum staff Utzon could cope with was six or seven; when the office grew to a dozen, he was unable to control the designers to the degree that his perfectionist personality demanded. This work method was exacerbated by Utzon's need to continually chew over problems and to revisit earlier solutions as the design developed in his search for perfection. When he was happy, he would announce to the engineer or the committee, 'I have solved the problem!' but in many cases he had solved it in his own mind and in his sketches – the detailed work still had to be carried out by others.

The problem was that there weren't enough 'others' in Stage 3. In the two previous Stages, Arups produced all the documentation and working drawings, but the different arrangements between architect and engineer for the interiors meant that Utzon no longer had that resource to fall back on. He continually refused all proposals that he should seek another architectural firm who could help him out. He was offended when Davis Hughes tried to ascertain from the RAIA how these resources might be provided and, at the time of the resignation crisis, he refused to consider any devolution of responsibility for non-design elements of the architect's role. Why he should have been so adamant is something of a mystery, except that the political pressures of the resignation saga and pressures from the Bring Back Utzon campaigners reduced the likelihood of compromise.

Originally, Utzon had entered the competition with the Swedish architects, Erik and Henry Andersson, with whom he had worked on a number of projects. The Anderssons came from a long line of builders and Erik accompanied Utzon on his first and victorious visit to Sydney in 1957, but disappeared from the scene soon afterwards. The Australian architect, Os Jarvis, visited Hellebæk in 1960 and for a time it was thought that he would set up a representative office in Sydney, but nothing happened. Following the resignation, when Utzon believed he might be recalled, he discussed with Seidler the possibility of Seidler assisting on the completion of the interiors. When the lawyer representing the Zurich Schauspielhaus arrived in Sydney shortly after Utzon's resignation to find out what had happened on Bennelong Point, he was surprised to discover that Utzon was resisting demands that he seek additional architectural assistance because they had negotiated just such a deal with him in Zurich. When there was talk in 1967 of Utzon returning to Sydney, he announced he would be quite happy working with Hall and his team.

In 1970, Utzon won a limited competition for the design of the National Assembly in Kuwait. Leslie Martin, one of the Sydney Opera House competition judges, advised the Kuwaitis on the selection of architect. Martin was determined there would not be a repeat of the problems in Sydney and wrote in the assessors' report that:

'It is first of all essential, in our opinion, that there should be a committee of management for this work which could represent Parliament on all questions of accommodation and costs; also that there should be one individual who would represent the Government so far as Mr Utzon is concerned.'

The report then went on to say: 'Mr Utzon's office is in Denmark. We suggest that he should be asked if he is prepared to work with a collaborating firm of his own choice from Kuwait or the Region. The object of this is to find a collaborating firm that could assist with production of Contract work and supervision and also costing and Quantity Surveying.'

Whatever amount of work in Sydney that might have been carried out by subcontractors in the detailing of the interior fit out and the construction of the glass walls, could Utzon's office of, at its height, some 16 people, a multicultural band of very bright but inexperienced designers, cope with the volume of work involved in a project of this scale? Their difficulties were exacerbated by the fact that they had to absorb major client changes, political interference and a fixed structural volume. In addition, they were trying to build Stage 3 in a way that was novel to the Australian construction industry using prototypes, subcontractors and factory production. This approach was Utzon's way of getting the quality of finish he required – a quality he did not believe he could get on site in Australia.

According to Wheatland, Utzon discussed taking on more people 'ad nauseam' but concluded that the team could complete the project 'give or take a few bodies'. Wheatland does however feel that Utzon had 'failed to sell the concept of his methodology to the bureaucracy, a tall order in those days given the conservative nature of the building design industry'.

In depth experience was a major problem for Utzon's office. He himself had not worked on a project of this size or indeed of any sort of theatrical or acoustic design. The exquisite set of houses at Kingo did little to prepare the office for the rigours of a major project like the Opera House. The lack of experience was exacerbated by the fact that three of his most senior staff, Paul Schouboe, Knud Lautrup-Larsen and Aage Hartvig Petersen, chose not to follow Utzon to Sydney. Jakob Kielland-Brandt, Mogens Prip-Buus, Jon Lundberg and Oktai Nayman, who did go to Sydney, were young and relatively inexperienced. Less than a year before Utzon's resignation, Jon Lundberg had resigned and returned to Denmark, as had Olaf Skipper-Nielsen who had been Utzon's representative in Sydney since 1959, and Kielland-Brandt was suffering from serious high blood pressure. They had worked for six years on the interiors and the glass walls and had not got near to solving the problems. It is a very patient politician indeed – one might say an irresponsible one – who would stand by and not review the management of a major expenditure of public money on a project such as the Opera House.

That is what politicians do; one of their most important roles is the allocation and the control of the expenditure of public money. It was perhaps naïve of Utzon not to fully understand their part in the process, but political savvy is one of the skills that the successful architect of major projects must have in his armoury. It was always thus from Christopher Wren to Norman Shaw to Norman Foster.

Today Utzon places the blame for his departure fairly and squarely on Davis Hughes. 'If we didn't have Davis Hughes we could have continued' he says 'He was a terrible man. But then, he could have pulled the whole thing down but he didn't. It was sure that Davis Hughes did not want me to continue.'

That may well have been the case by the beginning of 1966, but Hughes started out with a more positive view. At the first meeting with Utzon after

Hughes became Minister, the architect agreed to a 'timetable of availability of plans and specifications' on which contracts could be called. Hughes' note of the meeting says 'General tenor of the meeting satisfactory'. It was the non-delivery of these agreed items that altered the Minister's mood.

Writing in the *Sydney Morning Herald* in January 1995 at the time of the 'Unseen Utzon' exhibition, Davis Hughes admitted that he was 'relieved' when Utzon resigned. In the article he made public his frustrations with Utzon's production of drawings and the shortfall in accommodation. He praised the work of Hall Todd and Littlemore, seeing this as proof that Australia did not need 'distant icons' to design its major buildings, and he put down the criticisms of the completed building to 'a dogged coterie of Eurocentrics whose noses have been put out of joint by having prophesies of disaster for the Opera House on Utzon's departure proved hopelessly wrong. They just can't accept that fellow Australians can be up with the world's best.'

Davis Hughes clearly had no regrets at losing the integrity of a complete building created by one hand. It is not something that he saw as an issue. He acted with unnecessary haste when he called in the Architects' Panel, but as far as he was concerned he did not want Utzon on the job. He would have grudgingly accepted him back under the terms offered at the Lane Cove Motel meeting, but was doubtful if the arrangement would have worked. Once Utzon had left the country the door was firmly closed.

While the Minister was happy to see the back of his architect, it was hard to drum up support for Utzon amongst those involved with the project on the ground. Ove Arup and Zunz were willing to go to great lengths to see Utzon reinstated; Lewis was more cautious and felt that the firm should keep out of the argument. Farmer, the Government Architect, was prepared to accept Utzon's resignation in the hope of pressurizing him into accepting a new management structure, but it came as a shock to him that Utzon would rather make his resignation permanent than accept the role of design consultant. Corbet Gore, with the responsibility for construction, felt the 'log jam had cleared' when Utzon went. He was pressing Utzon just as hard as Davis Hughes for a programme of drawings for Stage 3 in the months leading up to the resignation. Even members of SOHEC were wavering. 'Silent' Stan Haviland told Utzon there was a split in the committee when Utzon telephoned him on 10 March 1966. On 24 March, Utzon requested Haviland to call a meeting of the Technical Advisory Panel, which Haviland did, but Utzon did not turn up.

Professor Ashworth was staunch in his support, although Utzon had suggested otherwise. On 27 April 1966, he wrote to Utzon:

'I have, in fact, done everything possible to try and persuade the Government not to let you go in this way ...I am indeed sorry if you feel you have any reason to believe otherwise, though the fact that you have not even replied to my phone calls ...would appear to confirm this. However, in my book, friends of ten years' standing should not be treated in this way without any explanation ...you expressed a wish to meet the Panel and Committee before you left, and I was sorry you did not come to the last meeting of the Panel, which had no business and was specially arranged to meet you.'

It was inserting the Major Hall into the existing shell that provided Utzon with his most intractable problem. There was just not enough space. Placing the two theatres side-by-side had restricted the width of the halls, but the decision to change the geometry meant that Utzon lost some 141,258 cu ft (4,000 cu m) of space. In his attempts to deal with both the acoustics and the seat numbers, Utzon was driven to compromise his designs. He was forced to raise the seats above the concrete banking using a separating steel structure. There was no other option, but it represented the sort of solution that he disliked as being 'dishonest', as did the original shell solution proposed by Ronald Jenkins using two skins of concrete separated by a steel structure and, uncannily, the mirror of the steel and ply solutions proposed by Lewis for the auditoria ceilings which were stoutly rejected by the architect. The difficulties of inserting so much into so little space meant that the vision of a 'perfect opera house' was starting to dissolve before his eyes.

Utzon's desire to build the perfect opera house was an important driver for the project. To achieve perfection, he was willing to scrap work, to rethink his ideas, to continually refine his designs. He sought perfection in the form of the building as well as its finishes. This approach inevitably extended the period of design and construction and it clearly had an impact on costs. But once the shell volume was fixed, there were too many competing elements for all of them to be perfect. All architecture is an intricate juggling act of form and function, at Sydney, the fixed size of the shells meant that the juggling was done with one hand tied behind the designers' backs. Whereas Peter Hall told the client it was impossible to fit all the requirements into the space available, Utzon failed to do so.

The changing relationship with Arups increased Utzon's isolation. In the first two stages, the engineers had not only designed the structures but they had managed the contract for Utzon, a role they took on willingly at the start in order to help him out although they were not being paid for it. Arups were responsible for paying the other consultants, but Utzon was hiring and firing them. Arups felt they had all the responsibility but little power and when work started on the interiors, which were more architectural and less structural than the first two phases, they wanted to change their relationship with the project.

The letters and memos setting out Arup's and Zunz's thoughts on the new arrangements arrived in Sydney just as Utzon and Lewis were settling in – it was not a good start.

Zunz was already annoyed that Utzon closed down his office for three months at the time of the move – creating a hiatus of almost twice that period – at a crucial time in the contract. His annoyance was exacerbated by the fact that Arups were left holding the baby with the frustrating and unproductive arbitration with Civil and Civic over the costs of the construction of the podium. In addition, during Utzon's absence, Arups were forced to take a series of 'architectural' design decisions in order to keep to the programme, some of which Utzon wished to revisit on his arrival in Sydney, adding to Arups' irritation in London and on site.

However difficult the first few months were, it is hard to understand how Utzon could have interpreted the Arup proposals to change the contractual relationship as an attempt to supplant him. His poor grasp of English and his lack of interest in contractual matters were possible contributory factors. He may well have been miffed by the underlying suggestion that he would continue to require management support. He clearly believed that he could carry out this stage on his own.

If Utzon had got on better with Lewis, the story may well have been very different. The clash of personalities has been cited as a key factor in the arguments that led up to the resignation. Lewis was a no-nonsense engineer who said what he thought, and who became frustrated with the lack of progress on the design of Stage 3. But such rows are not uncommon in the fraught atmosphere of a major building project. The problem was that Utzon still needed Arups, or someone like them, to carry out the huge amount of documentation work that needed to be done. He needed people to do drawings just as Arups had done the drawings for the first two stages.

But Utzon did not want Arups' help. He had stated in June 1963 that he was free to choose other engineers should he wish to. The fact that he criticized Arups for not making design suggestions in their report on the ceilings in 1965 is unfair since he was using Symonds' engineer, Peter Miller, to advise on the plywood structures – he couldn't have it both ways. If anyone should have looked at changes to the structure to make it work it was Miller, although Miller later disclosed that he had not been in full possession of the facts regarding the shell structures when he made his comments on the auditoria ceilings.

It is telling that at the late stage of his disagreements with Lewis, Utzon turned to Ove Arup to intervene, just as he had at the stalemate over the design of the shells with Jenkins in 1961. But in contrast to 1961 when Arup went against the advice of his team and sided with Utzon, this time he backed Lewis's judgement. Arup believed that the steel supported plywood ceilings in the halls looked the same and were more practical than Utzon's huge beams. Arup's rejection added to the architect's isolation and his bitterness is reflected in the letters to Arup following the resignation.

Despite the painful letters from Utzon, Arup personally continued to press for Utzon to be reinstated, to be in charge of design, although he thought it perfectly reasonable that he should pass on the role of supervising construction. Richard Weston in *Utzon* says that Arups denied the architect the support that 'conceivably might have saved him.' Utzon did have Arup's support, however Arup did not believe that his firm should resign from the job as the Utzon's supporters suggested. Arup believed it was acceptable for the engineers to resign if the architect had lost faith in them in order for him to appoint an alternative firm; he did not feel it was acceptable to resign in order to pressurize their client into a certain position.

Weston repeats accusations that 'business interests' took over and Arups remained in post. In fact, in terms of 'business interests' the partners believed that their future as a practice in Australia was likely to be hurt more by staying on the job than resigning; they realized that many of those supporting the Utzon campaign were just the bright, young architects they would be depending on in the future for commissions. If, as Weston says, Arups were swayed by business interests then the easier route would have been to resign. But they were directly contracted to the client , to resign would have further jeopardized the project and Arups had no quarrel with the client. More extreme suggestions that Arups produced the report on the plywood ceilings to discredit Utzon in the eyes of the Minister and to give him an excuse to fire Utzon are nonsense. By staying on Arups did, however, improve their financial position; up to the time of the resignation they had lost money on the job, by the time the building was completed the Opera House account was safely in the black.

Zunz and Arup were bitterly attacked when they visited Sydney in April 1966 for not resigning and were shouted down by an angry audience when Arup tried to explain his position. But having determined not to reveal the full scale of the problems, any defence was unconvincing to a group zealously convinced that full reinstatement of the architect was the only solution.

Zunz believed at the time that, '...if Utzon cares for the job more than himself he must compromise on all or every issue except the design of the building [but] if he persists in this uncompromising stand our position is clear – we must support the job to the full however difficult this may be.'

In Arup's own comment on the affair written in 1967, he says: 'The indisputable fact is that I – and this goes for most members of my firm – have lost confidence in Utzon, and that without this we could not resign on his behalf.' Arup suggested that this does not conflict with his earlier descriptions of Utzon as 'the best architect I have ever worked with' – he referred to Utzon's handling of space, forms, texture, colour and light. When Arup got to Sydney after the resignation, he found that things were even worse than he had feared: 'It would have been quite wrong to resign and thus publicly support Utzon in a matter where right was not on his side.'

Perhaps it was a mistake at the time that Arup and Zunz, when under attack by the Bring Back Utzon campaigners did not give chapter and verse of the problems as they saw them. Published a year after the resignation, Elias Duek-Cohen's tract *Utzon and the Sydney Opera House* highlights four accusations against Utzon: he was insisting on the wrong organizational approach; he ignored questions of time, he ignored questions of cost; and, he was not a practical man.

The most critical point was to do with organizational approach. It is clear that Utzon himself should have dealt much earlier with problems of design development and drawing production. His defenders point to the Government's refusal to permit the construction of prototypes, yet this ignores the fact that meeting after meeting, drawings were promised which never appeared. SOHEC's decision to reject proposals for 1,000 seats behind the orchestra clearly created great problems for the architect but, equally clearly, Utzon's small team could not provide the drawing power required to meet the Minister's demands.

In a meeting between the consultants, contractors and Davis Hughes, called immediately after Utzon resigned, Corbet Gore of Hornibrook commented that, although Utzon's programme showed a start on Stage 3 in June 1965, there were no documents available and it would be months, if not years, before there were.

In the three years he had been in Sydney, Utzon failed to find a substitute for Arups for the production of drawings and documentation – either in the form of additional staff or compliant subcontractors.

Utzon was confident he could manage Stage 3, but his attitude to management was cavalier. Writing to Ove Arup in February 1964 he wrote 'Management is in a way the easiest part of the job, something which most people can learn.' In Australia the construction industry was used to far greater documentation and detail than Utzon provided. According to Frank Matthews, who worked with Julius Poole and Gibson, the electrical consultants, from July 1964: 'In Australia we are used to things being itemised down to the last nut and bolt. Utzon always had a solution to a problem but he didn't put it down on paper; we would go out to lunch and he would sketch on the tablecloth and we would take the tablecloth home.'

Matthews found it refreshing to work with an architect who wanted to break new ground; 'We used to say "This isn't the way we do things in Oz" and Utzon would reply "Well, that is the way we will do it – we're here to nudge forward the frontiers of science." He was always changing things, nothing was ever finalised, but each change was an improvement.' Such a moving target, complicated by disagreements with Arups and Davis Hughes' delays in allocating funds for the plywood mock ups made forward planning a complex business. Bill Wheatland had been working on a Critical Path computer program with the help of IBM and Americans working at the Pine Gap joint defence facility and satellite tracking station in Western Australia. But there were too many imponderables for it to be of much use.

The shifting relationship with Arups reflected a changing attitude in Utzon himself; when he and Ove Arup worked so intensely on the geometry of the shells in Hellebæk, Utzon would say to him that it did not matter who designed what. 'You used to say,' Arup wrote to Utzon in April 1966, shortly after the resignation, 'at the beginning of our collaboration that architects should be anonymous, that it did not matter who did it, as long as it was done rightly [sic]. I realize that you have moved a long way from this attitude. A little humility is needed on your part.' Accreditation seemed unimportant as the great curving shapes were defined through many hours of argument, debate, sketching and calculation. When Utzon got to Sydney his tune changed. Perhaps he realized that the building was going to become a major architectural success and feared others taking the credit, but any suggestion of design collaboration was out. From then on it was 'only I' who could design the Sydney Opera House. It marks the shift in the Arup/Utzon relationship which reached its climax with Utzon accusing Arup in May 1966 of suggesting that he was merely hanging his designs on Arup's structure.

When the RAIA blamed some of the problems of the Opera House on the fact that Arups had a direct contract with the Government, it reflected an outdated role of the engineer prevalent in Australia at the time – that the engineer merely calculated the forces on drawings supplied by the architect and advised on the size of structural members. Such a role worked perfectly well in the simple world of post and lintel architecture, but the increasingly complex nature of modern architecture required a more creative input.

Utzon claims that he was warned by Sir Basil Spence and Sir William Holford (later Lord Holford) that Arup would try to steal the credit for the Opera House, and is of the view that Arup's Danish engineering training in Copenhagen instilled the idea that the engineer was superior to the architect. It is certainly true that Arup was not shy of publicity and that he believed in due credit for the work of the engineer, something that Spence and Holford, practising in a period when the architect was the undisputed leader of the building team, might well have thought inappropriate. Spence had, in fact, regularly used Arups as engineers, most notably on the designs for Coventry Cathedral, and was on the RIBA Jury that selected Arup for the Royal Gold Medal for Architecture in 1966 – but was very hurt when Arup failed to mention him in his acceptance speech. Nevertheless, the nomination of Arup for the Gold Medal and the fact that it was the second award to an engineer in seven years – Pier Luigi Nervi received the Gold Medal in 1960 – reflected architects' growing appreciation of engineers' contribution to their work.

One of the reasons sometimes cited for Utzon's belief that Arup wanted to take the Opera House job from him was the setting up of the multidisciplinary practice of Arup Associates, which integrated architecture, engineering, cost consultancy, urban and product design within one design studio in order to provide an operating example of Arup's concept of total architecture. There was no plan to encroach on work being carried out by the engineering side of the business, but Utzon was not the only architect to react to this competition. A number of leading architects – including Denys Lasdun, who was then working on the National Theatre in London – complained to Arup when they heard of the creation of Arup Associates.

While in the last half century the management of the design and construction process and the roles of the various consultants have become more collaborative, there has been a rise in the prominence of the 'star architects' who are invited to create signature buildings that become globally recognized landmarks of the host city or country. While the creation of great civic monuments is nothing new, this is the first era when architecture has been called upon to respond to the demands of the global competition of cities for tourism, business and 'branding'. While the jurors for the Sydney Opera House competition were well aware of the impact the design might have internationally as a piece of architecture, they could have little imagined the iconic status it would attain as a part of Brand Australia. The burghers of Bilbao knew exactly what they were doing when they commissioned Frank Gehry to design the Guggenheim Museum, but even so were astonished at the scale of the effect it had. Overnight the struggling Basque port was transformed into a global cultural honeypot; then every city wanted one.

As Joe Cahill's successors struggled with the political implications of escalating costs, they would not have known that the investment would be paid back many, many times over in terms of tourism, goodwill and national confidence. Even so, in a period when the effect of the iconic building was less well understood, the remarkable thing about the contract is not that the Government attempted to control the project when they did, but that they let things go on as long as they did.

It is, of course, an architectural tragedy that Utzon was not able to complete the interiors of the building and that we are unable to experience the building as he intended, yet many of the criticisms of the Hall interventions, such as the encroachment of the auditorium into the side aisles and the 'tusks' on the glazed walls on the north façade, were products of the problems of fitting the required accommodation within a fixed volume of space – problems that Utzon himself had not solved at the time of his departure. When Hall started work on the project he fully expected to build Utzon's designs, and this was the spirit in which he approached the job.

Hall's role in the saga of the Opera House has received considerable criticism from Utzon's supporters. While one can understand that they were

Dame Edna Everage wears the Opera House with pride at Ascot, 1976.

angry at failing to convince the profession to black the Opera House without Utzon in charge, their political position would seem to have affected any chance of balanced architectural comment from that quarter.

When Hall accepted the job, the problems were perceived to relate largely to execution; Utzon had claimed that designs were well advanced – Hall and his partners' job was to build it to Utzon's design. It soon became clear that this would be impossible because of the lack of the required number of seats and the ABC's revised brief.

The architect Glenn Murcutt – winner of the Pritzker Prize in 2002, the year before Utzon won it – mourns not just the loss of integrity of the final assemblage, but also the loss to Australia of the technology and techniques that Utzon was promoting. 'The country lost the potential of raising the level of architecture internationally, it lost the potential of a dozen or more great buildings from Utzon and it lost the technology that he was developing. The Government did a stupid thing.'

Utzon today says that he is 'absolutely grateful' for what he was asked to do. As are we all. The Opera House is proof that the age-old qualities of great architecture – of suitability to its site, the response to light, the creation of space, the scale and proportion, and the use of materials – are priceless assets that can repay their investments many times over. It is a concept that is hard to sell in our short-termist age. But every Sydney commuter ferrying in to Circular Quay whose day is kick-started by the thrill of the morning light glinting off those lizard-skinned shells and every tourist attracted to that beautiful city by Utzon's iconic shapes can thank Joe Cahill for his vision and daring. *Ars longa, vita brevis.*

BIBLIOGRAPHY

Baume, Michael *The Sydney Opera House Affair* with epilogue by Peter Hall (Sydney, Thomas Nelson (Australia) Ltd., 1967)

Curtis, Robert Emerson *A Vision Takes Form* (Sydney, Reed, 1969)

Drew, Philip *The Masterpiece: Jørn Utzon, A Secret Life* (Sydney, South Yarra, Hardie Grant, 1999)

Drew, Philip *Sydney Opera House* (London, Architecture in Detail series, Phaidon Press, 1995)

Drew, Philip *Utzon and the Sydney Opera House: As It Happened 1918–2000* (Sydney, Inspire Press, 2000)

Duek-Cohen, Elias *Utzon and the Sydney Opera House – A Statement in the Public Interest* (Sydney, Morgan Publications, 1967)

Frampton, Kenneth *Studies in Tectonic Culture* (Cambridge, Mass, MIT Press, 1995)

Fromonot, Francoise *Jørn Utzon: The Sydney Opera House* trans. Christopher Thompson (Corte Madera, CA: Electa/Gingko, 1998)

Giedion, Siegfried *Space, Time and Architecture* (Cambridge, Mass. and London 1941)

Gilling, Ronald *Utzon, The Institute and The Sydney Opera House* (Unpublished manuscript)

Hubble, Ava *More than an Opera House* (Sydney, Landsdowne Press, 1983)

Jordan, Vilhelm Lassen *Acoustical Design in Concert Halls and Theatres: A Personal Account* (London, Applied Science Publishers, 1980)

Messent, David *Opera House Act One* David Messent Photography (Sydney, 1997)

Mikami, Yuzo *Utzon's Sphere: Sydney Opera House – How it was Designed and Built* Photographs by Osamu Murai (Tokyo, Shokokusha, 2001)

Nobis, Philip *Utzon's Interiors for the Sydney Opera House: the Design Development of the Major and Minor Halls 1958–1966* A dissertation for the University of Technology, (Sydney, 1994)

Ove Arup Partnership *The Arup Journal* October 1973, Sydney Opera House Special Issue (London, 1973)

Prip-Buus, Mogens *Letters from Sydney* (Hellerup, Edition Bløndel, 2000)

Rice, Peter *An Engineer Imagines* (London, Ellipsis, 1993)

Smith, Vincent *The Sydney Opera House* (Sydney, Paul Hamlyn, 1974)

Utzon, Jørn *Sydney Opera House: Utzon Design Principles* (Sydney Opera House Trust, 2002)

Sowden, Harry *Sydney Opera House Glass Walls* (Sydney, Self published, 1972)

Weston, Richard *Utzon: Inspiration, Vision, Architecture* (Hellerup, Edition Bløndal, 2002)

Yeomans, John *The Other Taj Mahal* (Camberwell, Longman, 1973).
Ziegler, Oswald *Sydney Builds an Opera House* (Oswald Ziegler Publications, 1973)
Zodiac, No 5, 1959
Zodiac, No 14, 1965

Films & video recordings
Clouds: Jørn Utzon / a film by Pi Michael. [Denmark]: Fakta, 1994

The Edge of the Possible: Jørn Utzon and the Sydney Opera House. Directed by Darly
    Dellora. Produced by Sue Maslin. Written by Daryl Dellora and Ian Wansbrough.
    Australian Film Finance Corporation and Film Art Deco Productions, 1998

Job No 1112: Sydney Opera House / NSW Government and Ove Arup & Partners;
    produced by Collings Productions, Sydney, 1967

Sydney Soap Opera House: Produced by Uden Associates. Executive producer Patrick Uden.
    45 minutes.

Archival sources
NSW Public Works and Services
Sydney Opera House files c.1962–1975 and architectural plans. Includes original
    competition drawings submitted by Jørn Utzon.

State Library of NSW. Jørn Utzon records 1956–1967. Files from Utzon's Sydney office,
    including manuscripts, pictures, architectural drawings and models. Guide to the
    collection at ML MSS 2362/1

Oral histories from the Dennis Wolanski Archive of the Sydney Opera House. Davis
    Hughes, Corbet Gore, Charlie Weatherburn, Bob Kelman, Ted Farmer

Ove Arup & Partners. Company Archive

Churchill College Cambridge. Ove Arup Archive

Interviews
Jørn Utzon, Sir Jack Zunz, Sir Davis Hughes, Michael Lewis, John Nutt, Ian McKenzie,
Bob Kelman, James Thomas, Elias Duek-Cohen, Ken Woolley, Warwick Mehaffey,
Professor Henry J Cowan, Corbet Gore, Povl Ahm, Derek Sugden, Peter Smithson,
Christopher Johnson, Rafael Moneo, Frank Matthews.

Photo credits

Frontispiece Martin Sharp
Cover, pages 134, 143 David Messent
Page 3 Australian Consolidated Press Library.
Page 14 Color Prints
Pages 26,32,42,55,56,58,121,123,128 Arup
Page 35 RIBA Drawings Collection
Page 85 Australian News and Information Bureau
Pages 50, 54, 112 Max Dupain
Page 98 Fairfax Photo Library
Page 155 Syndication International.

Whilst all reasonable efforts have been made to contact all copyright owners, the passage of time has, in some cases, rendered this impossible. Those we have not been able to trace but seek fair and reasonable copyright fees are invited to contact the Publisher.

INDEX